The
NAMES
of the
STARS

ALSO BY PETE FROMM

If Not for This

As Cool As I Am

How All This Started

Night Swimming

Blood Knot

Dry Rain

King of the Mountain: Sporting Stories

Monkey Tag

Indian Creek Chronicles: A Winter Alone in the Wilderness

The Tall Uncut

THOMAS DUNNE BOOKS
St. Martin's Press
New York

The
NAMES
of the
STARS

| A LIFE IN THE WILDS |

Pete Fromm

THOMAS DUNNE BOOKS.
An imprint of St. Martin's Press.

THE NAMES OF THE STARS. Copyright © 2016 by Pete Fromm.
All rights reserved. Printed in the United States of America. For information,
address St. Martin's Press, 175 Fifth Avenue, New York, N.Y. 10010.

www.thomasdunnebooks.com
www.stmartins.com

Designed by Michelle McMillian

Tank Park Salute
Words and Music by Billy Bragg
Copyright © 1991 Sony/ATV Music Publishing Limited UK
All Rights Administered by Sony/ATV Music Publishing LLC, 424 Church Street,
Suite 1200, Nashville, TN 37219
International Copyright Secured   All Rights Reserved
Reprinted by Permission of Hal Leonard Corporation

Library of Congress Cataloging-in-Publication Data

Names: Fromm, Pete, 1958– author.
Title: The names of the stars : a life in the wilds / Pete Fromm.
Description: First Edition. | New York : Thomas Dunne Books, 2016.
Identifiers: LCCN 2016007365| ISBN 9781250101686 (hardcover) |
  ISBN 9781250101693 (e-book)
Subjects: LCSH: Fromm, Pete, 1958—Homes and haunts—Selway-Bitterroot
  Wilderness (Idaho and Mont.) | Authors, American—20th
  century—Biography. | Outdoor life—Selway-Bitterroot Wilderness (Idaho
  and Mont.) | Selway-Bitterroot Wilderness (Idaho and Mont.)—Biography. |
  Montana—Intellectual life—20th century. | Idaho—Intellectual life—20th
  century. | BISAC: BIOGRAPHY & AUTOBIOGRAPHY / Personal
  Memoirs. | NATURE / Ecosystems & Habitats / Wilderness.
Classification: LCC PS3556.R5942 Z469 2016 | DDC 818/.5403 [B]—dc23
LC record available at https://lccn.loc.gov/2016007365

Our books may be purchased in bulk for promotional, educational, or business use.
Please contact your local bookseller or the Macmillan Corporate and
Premium Sales Department at 1-800-221-7945, extension 5442, or by e-mail at
MacmillanSpecialMarkets@macmillan.com.

First Edition: September 2016

10 9 8 7 6 5 4 3 2 1

FOR MY PARENTS,
for opening the doors and letting me slip through

Acknowledgments

Many thanks to Oliver Gallmeister, who, over many camp-fires and on many rivers, worked with me on shaping this story, making me decide what it really was all about. And thanks, too, to Peter Wolverton, who pushed me to make it even more.

And to Sage, Pancoast, Rader, and all the other characters, named here and not, whom I've met along the way and who have each played their own far-beyond-supporting roles in my life. And, of course, to my families: my first, parents and siblings, and my second, Rose, Nolan, and Aidan, who bring me back from the wilderness.

Stories, stories, stories. A world and a land and
even a river full of the damn slippery things.

—RICHARD FLANAGAN, *DEATH OF A RIVER GUIDE*

The
NAMES
of the
STARS

1

North Fork of the Sun River
Bob Marshall Wilderness, Montana
May 2004

The storm seems, for a bit, to settle, a monotony of
squalls, the rain no longer quite streaming down as
if the sky itself were nothing but water. I dip low, peering
out the cabin window, studying the overcast, the thermometer's red column straining toward forty, the gusts cutting
across the meadow grass in waves. The lulls leave almost
silence, just the occasional pop of fir in the stove. Then the
rising beat of wind batters the cabin logs, and the drum of
rain skitters across the cedar shingles. Already after nine,
and weather regardless, still the ten-mile loop to check the
grayling eggs' progress, my daily chore. I shrug into the tired
rain gear, top and bottom both, adjust the jacket's hip zippers to leave the bear spray free, the handgun.

Out in the wind, the spray lashes in under the eaves, sting-
ing my cheeks, trickling into the start of my beard as I walk
around the cabin, raising each of the bear-proof shutters,

battening the hatches. All the routine. Then up the muddy track, over the hump and into the trees, toward the opening of the burn, the turn down toward the North Fork. Plodding, working up some heat, I watch the water bead off the oil I'd worked into my boots last night, watch my walking stick pock the mud, the cowbell I'd tied to its top all but silent with the easy rhythm. It's hood-up, head-down weather, little more than just the trail before my feet, until I start following bear tracks, last night's traffic, a reminder to keep my eyes up, to tuck the deafening hood behind my ears, to start making some noise. I sing, the only way I've thought of to constantly announce my presence, belting out "The noble Duke of York, he had ten thousand men . . ." as I enter the darker woods.

The rain, it turns out, instead of easing off, had only been warming up, and as I cross the pack bridge over the roiling brown North Fork, it comes down sideways, stupendously, stupidly hard, lashing the surface of the river to a froth. I lunge up the ridge toward the Spruce Creek eggs, laughing at just the wildness of it. Already soaked through, toes turned out in the mud as if herringboning up a ski trail, I make the ridge and cross the mile of recent burn, forgetting to sing to the bears, the blackened spear points of the trees easy enough to see through.

Until I reach the Hansel and Gretel stretch. Here the trail cuts into an older burn, dog-haired with fifteen-year-old lodgepole pine. Twelve feet tall and only inches apart, they're furred so tight to both sides of the trail—their needled branches threaded together, crowding in from both sides, whispering and shushing in the wind—it's more a green-walled tunnel than path. Even so, unable to see more than a few feet, unable to hear anything over the sighing and moaning of the trees, I don't muster up much more than a murmur myself, the pissing-down rain just too much, too loud. Who on earth would be out in this mess?

The sodden, impenetrable wall of pines an arm's reach to each side, I thump my walking stick against the occasional rock, rattling the cowbell, keeping time with Burl Ives, the Big Rock Candy Mountains, mumbling out "Oh, the buzzing of the bees in the cigarette trees, the soda water fountain. . . ." Working my way, again, through my old bedtime repertoire for the boys, the lyrics hammered into me through endless repetition.

I swing through the corkscrew bend near the drop down to the river, "where the lemonade springs and the bluebird sings," and there, two steps in front of me, lies a half-eaten elk calf. *Half*-eaten.

I stumble over myself, yanking off my hood. The calf lies spread-eagled on its back, gutted, a portion of the hams torn off from the inside, strings of meat limp against the ivory line of bone. Staggering back, I pull out my bear spray, push away the safety catch. With my other hand I unsnap my revolver's holster, wrap my fingers around its grip.

Another step back, another, rain running down my neck. No day-old calf can be more than a snack for a grizzly. Not something they'd eat part of and come back to. And even if it were, there's nothing scraped up over the kill, nothing hiding it as if the bear means to return.

I've chased it off. With the Big Rock Candy Mountains. Still stepping backward, I scan the trees, their dank, blank walls, seeing no more than four or five feet.

Rounding backward through the bend, bear spray out front, the calf disappearing behind the trees, I turn and walk, fast, back the way I'd come. I pound my stick, try shouting, "Coming through, make a hole, make a hole," what my dad said they were always shouting in the navy, barreling along the ship's tight corridors. At first my voice is hardly more than a squeak. I try again.

The Spruce Creek eggs are on their own today. And tomorrow.

I break out of the trees, glance down for tracks, finding only my own. Moving fast, able to see again, I look everywhere: across the short grass, the blackened rocks, up into the sooty burned snags, across the river's steep cut, up onto the burned clear face of the other side's cliff. I all but ski down the mud to the pack bridge and run up the opposite side, slowing for the dark timber of that bear highway. Shouting, "Kiss me goodnight and say my prayers!"—one song I never sang to the boys—I step carefully over the same tracks I'd walked over this morning, the rain drumming.

Rounding the cabin, I open the shutters, letting the gray murk leak in through the windows. Under the porch roof, the nesting robin blasts off by my face, and I let out a quick "Jaysis!" as if I'd been charged by a winged grizzly. Catching my breath, I unzip my rain gear, shake off what mud I can. Then I unlock the door and step inside as if my return had always been in doubt, lean back against it and take a long, deep breath. "Boys!" I call to the single, empty room. "I'm home!"

The bear had done me a favor, no doubt about it, slipping back into the pines, watching maybe, instead of challenging me for its kill. Or adding me to it. All its choice. I shake my head, the heat from the stove's banked fire taking away the chill, but not the shiver that runs through me.

I pick a log out of the wood box, open the stove, work it in over the coals. Then another. Latching the door, I stand back and pick a clean white splinter off the face of my wool shirt.

A month ago I'd been fighting to bring the boys in here with me. A monthlong campout. A wilderness experience they'd have for the rest of their lives.

Nolan, nine; Aidan, six. My sons. Neither one of them much bigger than that calf.

Nine and six. I realize with something approaching surprise that I'd only been a father for nine years. But what was I before? A kid myself for what? Seventeen years? And then off to college, the wilds of Montana, and then?

Plenty followed, I know, decades' worth, but all of it, everything I've ever done, or at least the reasons for it, when there were any, seem to have simply vanished. Before being a parent? There were just those first thirty-six years. And then Nolan. And Aidan.

Before—after.

But only nine years in, I've nearly fed them to the grizzlies. And, even so, I can hardly wish them here more.

2

Great Falls, Montana
April 2004

After moving to Montana at seventeen, I'd spent years dreaming of mountain men and their lonely, manly feats, of finding a cabin too remote to find, something off a postcard, a wolf hybrid, maybe, nosing out the door to savage all strangers. But instead I'd wound up in Great Falls, on the plains edged up against the spine of the Rockies, but not in the mountains themselves. A big, slow, muddy river backed up by dams stretched through town. Our house was an eighty-year-old Craftsman bungalow on a street lined with elms. I walked Nolan and Aidan, a third-grader and a kindergartener, back and forth from Roosevelt Elementary every day. Wild man become mild man.

In April, the sun barely warm, the trees just starting to bud out, the three of us kicked a rock along the sidewalk as I listened to stories of their day away from me when, a block shy of our house, a pickup wheeled around the corner and instead of straightening out, swerved straight at us, jerking to a stop only after bumping up against the curb. The boys stared as Steve, a fisheries biologist I knew, leaned out his window and grinned. "Hey," he said, "if you ever feel like getting a job, I might have just the one."

"Work?" I said. "Me?"

"We might need somebody to babysit grayling eggs up on the Sun. With your experience . . ."

I smiled. My winter with the salmon eggs, twenty-five years in the past, coming home to roost.

Still leaning out his window, he said the grayling thing would probably mean camping out for a month or so. He'd just left the first meeting about it, and details were sparse. "After your winter on the Selway, a month out in the spring should be a cakewalk," he said. "Right?"

The boys, shy at the best of times, clustered beside me, not missing a word. "What about these two?" I asked. If I was thinking at all, it was to hope they'd give us a wall tent. Set up alongside some deserted Forest Service road, a little creek, the boys splashing in the beaver ponds, making boats to throw into the rapids, bomb with rocks as they shuddered downstream. A little fishing. Bows and arrows. Chopping wood. Building fires. Enough visitors dropping by to keep them primed. All this in the first second or less. "They could come?"

"I don't know why they couldn't," Steve said.

I asked him to find out what he could and let me know. He nodded, an eyebrow raised as if he'd only been kidding, a one-liner about my extravagant employability.

He wheeled across the street to his driveway, done, but Nolan clamped onto my hand, just beginning. "Can we?"

"We'll have to find out more."

"But can we?"

"He didn't even know if they were actually going to do it. Or when. Or where."

"But if they do, can we?"

"We'll see."

"Even if they don't do it? Can we still go camping for a month?"

"Let's wait and see what he finds out."

"But can we camp for a month, no matter what? During school?"

They'd been to the Selway, Indian Creek, more than once. For years I'd had to tell them bedtime stories based on my winter there. The bobcat riding the deer over the cliff. The mountain lion leaping down a canyon. "We'll think about it," I said.

He gave me a look. *We'll think about it?* Worse than *We'll see.*

Aidan picked up a stick, wheeled left, right, testing its sword qualities. Nolan plugged along beside me. "Can we make moccasins if we go? Like the ones you made at Indian Creek? The ones that go up to the knee?"

"We can make those even if we don't go."

"It'd be better if we made them out there."

Out there. Wherever that was. Already planning with the same meticulous care as his father.

"We could make all our clothes out of deer skins," he said. The fall before we'd spent a staggering amount of time brain tanning an antelope hide, ending up with enough soft suede leather for a decent rag. We hadn't tackled deer hides yet, had no ready supply of deer skins, but, you know, details.

"We can chip flint for arrow points, kill a bird for the fletching. We'll start all our fires with flint and steel." He went on and on. All afternoon. All evening.

Last thing that night, in bed, story read, lights off, I leaned over for the hug and the kiss, and he said, "Can we?"

"I don't know, buddy. We'll see."

Even in the dark I could make out the roll of his eyes. *We'll see.*

Boys safely tucked in, I filled Rose in with the few details I had, ending as casually as I could, that if it worked out, it'd be pretty cool for them. She raised an eyebrow. "Grizzlies," she said.

"Grizzlies?"

"They're all over up there."

"That's like worrying about lightning."

"In spring? When they come out of hibernation? Starving? You in a tent with all your food? You might as well hang out a sign. *Dinner served nightly.*"

"We'd lock the food in the truck."

"If you're by a road."

"Well, yeah."

"They're snack-sized," she said, shaking her head.

Lions didn't thrill her much either. "The sneaky bastards." There were wolves out there, too. Fast, freezing water. Falls. Cuts. Illness.

I waved my hands, sang, "Lions and tigers and bears, oh my."

She stared.

3

Bob Marshall Wilderness, Montana
May 2004

With the fire roaring, I kick out of my boots, clumps of mud falling from the soles, dropping from my rain pants. I leave stark, bare prints on the oak floorboards as I slop my clothes over the drying wires above the stove, get dressed all over again, as if I could restart the day. I pull a chair up before the stove and hold my hands out, my fingertips a bit pruney.

My heart long since slowed, the grizzly rush fading out of me, I slump back, blow out a breath. My clothes steam on their wires, water dribbling down now and then, the drops hissing and dancing across the iron top of the stove, and I close my eyes to listen. Dozing maybe, a little, I wake to something: a change in the air, a sound, a movement. I sit up. The drumming of the rain's gone silent. I stand, step to the door, push it out. It really isn't raining.

Wisps of ground fog cling to the willows by the creek,

around the trees across the meadow, but above it almost seems that there are lighter spots, a thinning here and there in the clouds. I push into my drier boots, not bothering with the laces, and step into the novelty of dry air. I wander, eventually, to the woodpile, hooking the ax off the bunkhouse porch as I pass.

For the next hour the steady thunk of the ax, the dry fir leaping apart, the haul of armload after armload into the cabin keeps me occupied. I glance, only now and then, at the tree lines, for bears I don't really expect to see, and at the sky, for blue I have only fainter hopes of spotting. After my last load in, the wood box stuffed to bursting, I unlock the storage side of the bunkhouse, climb the ladder to the mouseproof platform, and retrieve the chocolate chip cookie mix I'd packed when I'd still been packing for the boys. "Treats tonight," I say, as if they're beside me, a habit I cannot break. "A we're-not-bear-shit-*yet* celebration."

Later, I pull the last batch from the stove, admitting, finally, how impossible this would have been, for me to push them through that Hansel and Gretel stretch day after day. But the smell of warm cookies filling the cabin, the sun, no lie, making an appearance minutes before dropping below the mountains, I can't help but wonder what a month like this, with the incubators within sight of the cabin instead of five miles away, no ten-mile daily loop to endure, would have been like with them. If it would have been something, like Indian Creek, that would have set them off on a trail they'd follow for life. And, if so, I wondered how many grizzlies would step back into the shadows to let them pass. Or not.

I set the cookies on the table, no one here to feast on them, and then I push them aside, unable to muster the appetite for a single bite. Not having even told Nolan I'd found a source for deer hides in Great Falls, had hidden some away in my packs before leaving. Now I pull them from beneath my bunk, spread them out on the table, and in the middle, tightly rolled, almost forgotten, are their T-shirts, patterns for the mountain-man wear I'd make for them out here. Nolan's Roosevelt Roadrunner, Aidan's Batman. They stop me cold.

It's just too easy to picture them inside the shirts, here in this cabin, tearing out into the rain, asking if they could put the next log into the fire, light the lantern, chop the wood. I sit for a while just watching the shirts before finally picking up my pencil, tracing around them, then reach for my knife, cutting out the fronts and backs, leaving the flank's wild tag ends edging the bottoms of their vests, pounding stitch holes around the perimeters. Instead of thread, just sewing them together, I light the lantern and cut miles of leather lacing to cross-stitch in an X pattern. Savage wear extraordinaire.

Surrounded by them, I pull my chair close to the fire, the rain once again drumming down, and they crowd in, watch me pull the laces tight, crossing the Xs. They get in my light. I swear I can smell them.

Great Falls, Montana
April 2004

Details trickled in over the weeks after meeting the fish biologist. There wouldn't be a road exactly. In fact, after the two-hour drive to the mountains, there'd be an open boat trip up Gibson Reservoir and then a full day on horseback, fifteen or twenty miles up the North Fork of the Sun River, all our gear packed on mules.

Though it was a little farther away, a little more isolated— kind of smack dab in the middle of the Bob Marshall Wilderness actually—there would be a cabin, a Forest Service wilderness guard station. A hard-sided, bear-proof domicile. I pushed that at Rose, and she pushed back. How could I possibly keep an eye on both of them around the clock? How far would we have to go every day to check on the eggs? How would I keep Aidan, the mad dash his preferred mode of travel, reined in? How could I possibly keep them entertained?

They were not TV watchers; we owned no Xboxes. The only play station they knew was their backyard. Just last year, heading to the Grand Canyon for a spring break, a friend gave us a pair of Gameboys for the ride. "It's the only way to go," she said, "with kids." I stuffed them deep into the back of a closet, never looked for them again.

I kept my eyes open for different kinds of things. Driving down an alley one day, I spotted a giant sawed-off butt section of a cottonwood tree, three feet in diameter, eight or nine inches thick. I hauled it home, built a tripod to stand it up, its tree rings pointed out toward the boys, a target for the hatchets they'd learned to throw, their gigantic mountain-man throwing knives.

In our backyard, I'd built a tree house, framing the floor into and around the crab apple's four main stems. Branches came up through the floor, out the sides, the roof. A slide exit, covered with PVC, made the sound barrier seem possible with every descent. Windows covered every approach: down the alley, toward the house, out the back toward the mysterious neighbor, Earl, who kept an eye on their antics.

One day the boys came in from the backyard, carrying several gleaming solid steel spheres, a bit bigger than golf balls. "What are these?" they wanted to know.

I took one, curled my fingers around it. Serious heft, a polished smoothness almost glassy. They were, I had to admit, cool. "Where did you find them?"

Aidan pointed. "Under the tree house."

A complete wrecking ball in the hands of most young boys. Either some clown distributing instruments of carnage to the neighborhood kids, or a Boo Radley, dropping treasures at the tree.

A pocket tackle box showed up one day. Another, some old lawn chairs with four-inch-tall legs. Perfect for the tree house.

When Nolan decided to make an atlatl—an ancient spear-throwing stick, a predecessor of the bow and arrow—for a science fair project, I caught Earl peeking out of his open garage door, watching us carrying the atlatl's five-foot-long darts, fletched with turkey tail feathers, out to the car.

He was there waiting for us when we returned from the park, Nolan's zinging fifty-yard shots with the darts. "Atlatl?" he asked, stepping into the alley, pointing toward the ancient throwing stick. Nolan nodded. "Like the mammoth hunters used?" Nolan glanced to me, like, *How does he know?* and nodded again.

Earl waved us into his yard, into his house, new territory for us all.

On a long table in his living room, underneath a television far bigger than ours, lay a six-foot-long, cordovan-brown arc, three to four inches thick. Not quite log, not quite ivory. "Mammoth tusk," Earl said. "Got that working up on the pipeline. They'd push up out of the tundra now and then. Had a bigger one, but couldn't get it back."

The boys stared as if confronted with pure gold. Earl said, "You can touch it." And they did, running their hands over the ancient curve, the spiderweb of cracks nearly too small to feel. I knew they pictured the whole animal, the living room packed and reeking with damp mammoth dreadlocks, pulsing with its oceanic breaths, the two of them facing it down with their suddenly tiny darts.

The following year, Nolan's scientific interest drawn to knights and castles, armor and blades, we sat sort of watching football games while we joined together countless little metal loops, making chainmail. An endless drudgery, something tailor-made for his uncanny attention span, he spun sheets of four-in-one mail, then a smaller piece, six inches square, of six-in-one—every ring connected to six others—the armor of the kings.

We took it all outside, pinned it to the hay-bale archery backstop, and he fired arrows into it. Lobbed spears at it. Then into a piece of elk rawhide. Then a sheet of steel we'd snuck out of the recyclers. Testing various armors of the age. Taking meticulous notes. From his garage, Earl watched.

The next day, the boys off at school, the doorbell rang and the back door cracked open before I started out of my chair, someone calling, "You home?"

Earl stood in the door holding a two-foot-long sword, gleaming steel, a hand guard, even a curved-back cutlass tip. "I thought he'd probably want to test all that armor against a sword, too," he said. "But, figured I better give this to you first, let you decide."

I touched my thumb to the edge, and he said, "Careful. I sharpened it."

He had indeed. I thought, *Seriously?* But he'd watched us stretch and scrape and brain tan an antelope hide under the tree house. He'd watched them throw knives, hatchets, come screaming down the tree house's slide holding any exposed skin away from the reentry burn. How much worse could a razor-sharp sword be?

Earl backed out of the doorway, started off for the alley. I followed, thanking him, then asked, "Did you leave some steel balls in the backyard once?"

He turned, smiling. "Ball bearings from the trains. Visiting some of the cronies at the shop, thought your boys might like them."

He used to work, I discovered, for the railroad, in the maintenance shops.

"Your kids," he said. "I wouldn't give this shit to my nephew for anything." He walked back to his garage, giving a wave over his shoulder.

I stuck the armor collection on the cottonwood block with nails. When they got home, the boys hacked away. Nolan took his notes. When it was time for the science fair, they wouldn't let him bring in the weapons. Just his results. He took second place. Robbed. "It would have been better with the weapons," he said.

At the foot of their beds they each had a tall bucket full of wooden swords I'd made for them, replicas of *Lord of the Rings* swords, knives, spears, bows, lances. Their weapons' buckets. A friend of mine, visiting for the first time, went into their room with them, pulled out a sword, said, "What's this?"

"My weapons' bucket," Aidan said, as if saying, *my bedspread* or *my shoes*, something as common as air.

My friend came back out, shaking his head. "Wish *I* had a weapons' bucket," he said.

In her bedroom, Rose had long rows of heart-shaped stones along her windowsill, across her dresser, Aidan's gifts.

In their room, along with the weapons' buckets, they had an aquarium sitting atop their old changing table. In it, a piece of lava rock from the Idaho fields, some crystal-embedded stones from the Pioneer Mountains. And a single bluegill. A perch. Both caught in a pond off the Missouri, an old gravel pit, bucket-stocked by persons unknown. We'd float the Missouri, then put out some worms and bobbers. They terrorized the population, and we had fish fry after fish fry before Aidan decided he wanted to keep some.

All winter long he fed them whatever bugs he found, but mostly night crawlers. Dangling them outside the tank, sweeping them slowly back and forth before the glass, he trained the bluegill, named Squiggles for the brilliant blue track patterns along his face, to leap up and take the worm from his fingers. A little Great Falls SeaWorld.

At another pond, he once caught an eight-pound carp on his three-foot-long Zebco. As he tugged and tugged, cranked and cranked, we figured he'd hooked a submarine. He was incensed when I released it, the biggest fish we'd ever seen. Later he caught a snapping turtle, was less upset about its release.

For the following year's science fair, continuing the medieval bent, Nolan dove into siege warfare and we built a trebuchet, a mechanically improved catapult.

We really didn't need any Gameboys.

Nolan could read for days, and Aidan liked to fish, but what if, out in the wilderness, the river was high, the fishing off? And, really, even if it wasn't, could that last a month?

But they'd been camping, running rivers, staying in Forest Service cabins since birth. I could teach them to fly-fish. We'd have the time. We'd bring cards, baseballs and gloves, deer-skins to sew (if I could find any); we'd make slingshots, bows and arrows. They'd scour the woods for perfect sticks, thousands of them (all without ever once getting out of my sight). We'd fashion enough swords and lances, knives and daggers, to keep down entire armies of Orcs. But a month? After the stroll out to the fish eggs, the other twenty-three-some hours to fill? Day after day?

And that stroll. Dave, the fisheries biologist in charge, said he'd *try* to keep the eggs within a mile or so of the cabin, but that he wouldn't really know until the snow melted and they could get in to choose their spots. But a couple of miles? The boys could manage that daily loop. That alone would give us something to do, a core to structure the day around.

Honestly, I worried more about the trip in than the daily walk. It'd start out great, the huge novelty of the horses, their old cowboy thrill, and I could almost picture Nolan enduring a day in the saddle, deadly serious. But Aidan I could barely picture sitting still at all, let alone enduring a day of it without deciding he was done. And all of this playing out in front of a bunch of horsemen, grizzled wilderness veterans who ate unruly children for snacks.

Offering some small degree of payback, I called my parents, as I had twenty-five years earlier to tell them I'd be spending the winter alone in a tent, in the wilderness, out of contact with the rest of the world. This time, I told them I'd be taking the boys.

"What?" my mother said.

I explained as much detail as I had.

"But what if they decide they want to go home?" she asked. "After a day or two? What if it rains the whole time?"

As kids, we'd spent weeks in a rented cabin on a Wisconsin lake watching the rain pour down. My parents, digging deep to find any source of distraction, took us out on car tours of Mineral Point, my mom reading historic details from her clutch of chamber of commerce guides. Then into the country, glaciation details recited to a station-wagon load of damp and desperate children: kettles and moraines and eskers, terminal ridges. The only high points were the humps in the old highway. My dad took them fast enough to leave our stomachs floating for an instant, the boys whooping, the girls groaning. That was a few days before everyone got sick, before evenings sank to my father sitting us one after another at the dining room table, having us tilt our heads back over the chair to say "Ah," while he gagged us with long-stemmed cotton swabs, painting our tonsils with purple gentian.

"It'd be another family vacation from hell," I said. "But they love camping. And if it rains, or they get sick of it, we'll deal with it."

"You'll have to," my dad said.

"It's just crazy," my mom said.

It went round and round as I thought, *I was just calling to let you know, not to ask permission,* until my dad said, "Well, let us know what you decide," not quite able to resist a chuckle. "It'll be an experience they'll never forget. One way or the other."

So, playing it both ways, I started to shop, to put aside things we could bring in with us for our month in the wilderness, all the while starting their baseball season, the spring ritual, me the coach for both their teams, though I set up other dads to take over, just in case. I scored big on Aidan's team when the grandfather of one of the other players picked up an overthrown ball and threw it back to me with a perfect knuckle ball. I raised an eyebrow, walked over, and asked who he was. "Jack," he introduced himself, but insisted he was just there to watch. He went on to talk about his years in minor league baseball, how he'd had to quit to raise his family. When I asked, he jumped at the chance to coach. He'd forgotten far more about playing baseball than I ever knew. At school, I talked to their teachers, who laughed at the idea that missing a few weeks of kindergarten and third grade should stand in the way of such an experience.

The idea had gotten quite a bit bigger than a campout beside a dirt road, but I'd also let it trickle a little beyond the "we'll see" stage. Maybe to the "maybe" level. Though I always added that we didn't know yet, that nothing was certain, I should have seen that as far as Nolan was concerned, it was all systems go, just a niggle of nervousness fraying the edges.

Then, only a week before they guessed we'd go, Dave called. The Forest Service was loaning the cabin at Gates Park to the Fish and Game. With the boys, questions of responsibility and liability had surfaced. Dave had worked his way successfully through the Fish Wildlife and Parks bureaucracy, but he'd just gotten off the phone with the

Forest Service district ranger, and true to everything I'd learned working in the Park Service, this person was unwilling to take on any whiff of liability. "I tried everything," Dave said. "Even said we could draw up some kind of waiver. He wouldn't budge. They won't let your boys go."

I stood staring at the phone.

Dave asked if I'd still go in, if it was by myself.

I told him I'd have to get back to him.

"Have you talked to them?" Nolan demanded. "What did they say?"

"They're worried about liability," I said, then tried to define liability to a nine-year-old.

"But nothing will happen."

"If it does."

"But the Fish and Game guys will say everything is their fault."

"They've got a policy about kids under twelve."

"Just because I'm not twelve?"

"They won't let their guys take their kids, so they say I can't take you."

"You don't even work for them. They could tell their guys that, so then you can bring us."

"I know, but—"

"Call the guy," he pleaded. "The district guy. If he's the one who says no, you might have to talk to him yourself."

I thought Nolan should be the one to talk to this district ranger. That he'd get the job done long before I could.

I'd have liked to have seen that bureaucrat squirm before him.

Nolan said, "I think you have to talk to that guy, Dad."

A woman asked, "Who's calling, please?"

She left me waiting a minute, then reported that the district ranger had just stepped out of the office but would call back.

The next day he was on the other line.

The next day out of the office.

The next day annual leave. Until after we were due to go in.

Nolan was rabid, dashing out of school every day, grabbing my arm, hanging there. "Well?"

"The district guy won't even talk to me," I told him. "He won't even return my calls."

"Keep calling."

"I am."

Nolan gave his odd muffled roar of ultimate frustration, kicked at the pea gravel.

At night I raged about this kind of line-toeing, rule-waving cog who had driven me out of the Park Service. But Rose said, "It just isn't going to happen. It was a crazy idea anyway."

I bristled at that *crazy*. Crazy? To let them run wild? To go so far beyond video games and role-playing to actually exist? To have this thing inside them forever that none of their peers would ever know?

I said, "Well, I can't see going without them. What would be the point?"

Rose looked at me. "The *point?* This is what you do, what you've always done. You can't keep putting everything off for them."

"I'm not putting anything off."

"But this is who you are," she said.

"Who I am?" I said. "What?"

"They'll survive without you. We will. You can't give up your whole life all the time."

"Give up my life? They *are* my life."

"But this is part of you, too. It's who you are. You need to do this."

I shook my head. Telling Nolan he couldn't go, but that I could? That was who I was?

"Besides, you already told Dave you'd do it. How's he going to find someone else now?"

I called Dave, asked one more time if he thought there was any chance, if a drive over to the ranger's house would do any good. A grenade maybe. He said no, not a chance, he'd tried already. Everything. I asked if they'd be screwed if I said I wouldn't do it. A silence stretched; then he said only that he'd understand.

I stood by my desk in the basement, the basement I'd finished by hand, matching the eighty-year-old trim upstairs. I'd made the file cabinets too, quarter-sawn oak, dovetailed drawers. Was that who I was? Above my desk, framed covers of the books I'd written, awards received, stretched along the wall. Who I was? In the guest bedroom behind me, the pelt of the bobcat that had gone over the cliff in Indian

Creek hung on the wall. On the bookcase sat the ancient skull of a buffalo I'd pulled from a crumbling cutbank on a Wyoming river. Who I was?

I took a breath and, letting it out, deflating, told Dave I'd go. For all sorts of vague reasons. Or none at all. Not letting him down? Not backing out? Plain old momentum? Because it was who I am? Or was?

Missoula, Montana
1978

When I graduated from high school in Milwaukee, Wisconsin, my parents gave me a calculator. A calculator. I've no idea what my twin brother got. Maybe another calculator. He was probably fine with it—a calculator was a bigger deal then, an investment, an off-to-college hope for academic achievement—but I couldn't even pretend. My parents made no comment about my reaction, other than to allow me to return it, take the money down to the sporting goods store, and buy a backpack instead. Something I'd really use. After all, I was going to Montana.

Montana. Chosen because I saw an application for it. Because I was already late in applying for anywhere. Because, on a more successful family vacation than our Mineral Point excursion, my parents had station-wagoned us out to the Tetons when I was twelve and, one evening, had loaded us onto a tourist float trip, crowded us in with other families on a raft the size of a barge, floated us down the Snake before those mountains at sundown. Because that river and those mountains jutting up out of the high plains still split the sky in my mind.

But when I'd landed alone in Missoula, a city I'd never heard of, in a giant state in which I knew exactly no one, at a college I knew nothing about, I pulled the campus map from the folder I'd been given and took off for the pool, the one place I figured would be like any other pool, a place to be cocooned in water, isolated, safe. The university's swim team being what it was, I was offered a scholarship. From my first day in Missoula, I swam day in, day out, mornings, nights, staggering through the wildlife biology core classes in between. Chemistry, physics, calculus, stats. All glimmered through a chlorine halo. All a bazillion miles from any soaring peaks or wild waters. I might never have left high school, or Milwaukee.

My second year varied only in my randomly selected roommate. I walked into my room hoping to be early enough to claim the best of the identical beds, desks, but found I'd arrived second. The roommate wasn't there, but his stuff was, everywhere, arranged as if by cyclone. And what stuff. A collection of the most outlandish gear: double-bitted axes, headlamps, rugged green jeans, and heavy yellow shirts, all sooty and scorched, a Smokey the Bear hat and gun cases, holding, I had to guess, guns, something I'd never seen in my life. The room reeked of stale woodsmoke tinged with mildew, old canvas, gun oil. I dropped my backpack, unzipped it, and pulled out my goggles, my miniscule Speedo, and was caught holding them when the door flung open, my new roommate, Rader, stepping in to eyeball me. I had to admit I was on my way to the pool.

But over the course of that year—Rader perched on his bed, reading aloud the most extraordinary feats from his nonstop diet of mountain man books—I was pulled into his world. Hugh Glass crawling hundreds of miles after being chewed up and spit out by a grizzly bear only left us wishing it could have been us. John Colter stripped naked by the Blackfeet, forced to run for his life through the prickly pear and sage, seemed the definition of luck. What had we done to be so cheated of such opportunity, such incredible stories?

The answer, we were forced to face, was that we'd been born too late, cheated by time. We'd never be mountain men, never be hounded by wolves, clubbed by Blackfeet, frozen to death beside a beaver pond, eaten by grizzlies. After my swim practice, we'd stalk to the food service, shuffle through the lines, fill and refill our trays, and wish we were hunkered over a campfire in one raging blizzard or another, chewing on moose meat or otter haunch, wolverine cheeks—something, anything wild. We'd go back for ice cream, nursing the injustice, the accident of our birth years.

Then, at the start of my third year in Missoula, time reversed itself. The university cut the swim team, and I was left with huge gaps in my day filled with nothing but an inordinate amount of unspent energy. Idle hands. Into this perfect storm walked a girl I'd taught lifesaving to the year before, strolling onto the deck of the Grizzly Pool, where I worked as a lifeguard. She'd heard about a job in the Idaho wilderness, the chance to spend seven months, an entire winter, alone, hunkered down in a wall tent beside the Selway River. Something to do with salmon eggs. She thought I might be interested. She held out the phone number of the game warden in charge. The figure of a goddess clad in nothing but a skintight, micron-thin layer of spandex stood right before me, but all I saw were bearded men on snowshoes pulling steel traps out of freezing black water. I called from the pool. The job was mine.

For the next two weeks I gathered supplies I bought more by guess than plan, and then the wardens picked me up and dropped me off in the Selway Bitterroot Wilderness, beside a channel holding two and a half million salmon eggs. It was the middle of October. I'd just turned twenty. The wardens would retrieve me in June, once the eggs I babysat were hatched and on their way to the Pacific.

My stuff, I wasn't even really sure what it all was, sat in a pile in the middle of the tent. The puppy Rader had gotten for me on the last day, Boone, sniffed around the canvas corners, then stepped out into the world, a world much bigger and much emptier than it had been the day before.

We were in for the long haul. Me and a six-week-old dog. Mountain men. That first day alone, and for many after, I'd have given anything at all to be back in a dorm room, just a college kid. A swimmer even.

Weeks passed, months. Ice clamped down on the river, the snow piled higher and higher. And higher. The thermometer fell. Zero. Ten below. Twenty below. Forty. Every day my sole duty was to keep water moving through the channel, but every night the waterfall at the channel's end froze solid, stopping the water, threatening to freeze the entire thing, leaving me with two million little salmon cubes. So, every morning I chopped the frozen falls apart with an ax, letting loose the water trapped behind it, keeping it flowing, the eggs alive. It took, on a normal day, about five minutes. The rest of the day, every day, twenty-three hours and fifty-five minutes, was free time.

I lived through it. Learned how to. Learned that loneliness ebbs. Learned that a place like that, alone, becomes more than a place. That while I held absolutely no significance in that place at all, it became a part of me. A part of me it would take years, decades, to only begin to understand.

Twelve years later, surprising no one more than myself, I wrote a book about that winter, *Indian Creek Chronicles,* and that winter grew, caught on with people. In certain circles—Forest Service offices, Fish and Game headquarters, the host of people who both read and enjoyed the mountains—that winter became part of the lore. Not me, so much, but the winter, the place. Just as I would have had it.

And though it had taken some twenty-five years, in one Montana Fish and Game office, the story had circled all the way around, pulling me back in.

Great Falls, Montana
May 2004

The day I was to leave, solo now, the boys tumbled out of their beds, crawled onto my lap on the couch, their bodies prickly with heat. "Are you positive?" Nolan murmured.

"I'm afraid so," I said, my arms around them both.

From the back door, Rose cried, "Donuts!" and Aidan leapt, but Nolan only augered in more deeply.

I stood us both up. "Let's get you a maple bar," I said, and he leaned against me the whole way, slumping at last into his chair. They each had their own waxy bag, so my Fish and Game driver and I could split the dozen in the box. Rose's more-is-better style of graciousness.

While they dug in, I carried my packs to the edge of the front porch, my ride already half an hour late. The boys got dressed, came back out to sit with me on the couch. I had on a rough long-sleeve shirt, and over that a wool Pendleton of my dad's, age paring him down until he'd passed it along to me. Too hot inside, I rolled up the sleeves, glanced at the clock. Seven thirty. I wiped a flake of sugar glaze from the corner of Aidan's mouth. They'd stay as long as it took.

A gray pickup whistled past our house, the driver looking straight ahead, not searching for any address numbers. I didn't catch the Fish and Game's grizzly head logo, but I headed out, saw the truck stopped midstreet about three blocks down, just short of the school.

Behind me the phone rang and I heard Rose call, "It's him." The truck U-turned. The boys tumbled out the front door. "How come he's down there?" Aidan asked.

"He missed."

The truck climbed up over the lawn, fighting its way into our model-T driveway. A tall, lanky guy in his forties unfolded from behind the wheel. "They gave me the wrong address, or I wrote it down wrong, or something."

He introduced himself as Gags, and we shook hands, the boys dutifully following suit, mumbling hellos.

We dropped my packs over the side of the pickup, and he unscrewed the lid of one of the three Igloo coolers strapped in back. Beneath gallons of clear water, maybe an inch and a half of little pink BBs layered the bottom. I lifted the boys over the side, Gags pointing out the black spots in the eggs, the eyes. "They're pretty active," he said, and I wondered if I'd missed a joke.

You could have fit the entire load in a gallon jug, but they were what I was leaving the boys for, for longer than I'd ever left them. I lifted Nolan back down to the grass. Aidan.

Then, there we were, nothing left in the yard. Gags checked his watch. "Guess I'm a little late."

I stepped to Rose and gave her a hug. Same as twenty-five years before, in front of the dorms in Missoula. The boys crowded in, Aidan more serious than usual, Nolan gripping like he'd never let go, like this was his final plan, to go barnacle, stowaway.

I finally had to take a knee, pry his arms from around my neck. His eyes glistened. "I have to go," I said.

"Why?" he asked, and with nothing close to an answer, I kissed him once more, then stood and opened my door, shut it with a thunk between us.

Gags backed out of the drive as I rolled down my window. It was already eight, late for school, but the boys tore down the block after us, the tradition. I waved back from the passenger seat, and they stopped at the corner, screaming, "Bye! We love you!" tears streaming down Nolan's face.

We turned the next corner, the boys gone behind us, and I twisted around to face forward, to find a holder for my coffee cup, a place for the donut box, anything at all to keep my hands busy, my eyes averted. The truck was a mess: papers, jackets, dog hair. Gags threw something out of the second cup holder and waved me toward it. "Just got a reprimand for having my dog in the cab with me," he said, grabbing at some paperwork on the dash. "A *written* reprimand. That's Helena for you. Nobody with enough to do without looking for where somebody's dog finds a ride. He's not a big dog either. He prefers riding up front."

Hardly pausing for breath, Gags worked himself up over

inane anti-dog regulations, then the silliness of headquarters in general, then the drama of fisheries' politics and hatcheries and fish eggs. I wasn't tracking closely, just looking out the window, waiting until I thought I could trust my voice before asking, "So, have you ever made this trip yourself?"

He seemed almost startled to find me there in the truck with him. At least able to speak. "To Gates?" he said. "Yeah, I've been up there before."

"So, you're an old hand around horses?" I knew as much about horse travel as I did interplanetary flight.

"Me?" he said. "Horses? I know all I need to know about horses. They're big, they're dumb, and sooner or later they're going to hurt you."

He was off again, rattling off one horse disaster story after another, while I hunkered lower in the truck seat, the outer ramparts of the Bob Marshall Wilderness looming before me, the towering wall of the Rocky Mountain Front, storms mounting dark and low beyond them, gathering for their assault on the plains.

Interrupting himself, Gags assured me, "That's all you ever need to know about horses. They're big, they're dumb, and sooner or later—"

"They're going to hurt you," I finished, trying to smile.

"You got it," he said, snaking the truck up the cliff face. Hanging on the knife-edged crest for only a moment, we dropped down toward the lake, hidden until now, a sullen, flat expanse of water as green as the spruce surrounding it. I caught a glimpse of an open aluminum boat bumping against the rocky shoreline, a thickset hunch of dark rain gear huddled beside it. My guide for the next leg of a journey I was far from certain I wanted to take.

Gags pulled in and, after the weeks of phone calls, I finally met Dave. He leaned in over the side of the truck to check out the eggs, as happy, it seemed, to meet them as he was to meet me. He scooped a handful up out of each of the coolers, commenting on the size of the eye spots. "Pretty far along," he said. "You may not be out here long after all."

"What?" I said, but he only shrugged and loaded my month's worth of gear into his boat, the precious cargo of grayling eggs. After Gags and I got in, we headed out into the spine-jarring chop, loose bits of hay, the previous cargo, whirling around us. Rain spattered down. In a lull between gusts, I shouted, "How about you, Dave? You a horseman?"

He cut the throttle. "What?"

I waved it off, but we were already stopped, wallowing. I asked again.

"Horseman?" he said. "Me? Hell no."

Gags said, "Show him where the wreck was."

Dave pointed to the Lake Trail, a gray thread on the nearly vertical rock wall, maybe fifty feet above the water. "Next to that little break in the cliff," Dave said. "Kelly jumped off when it started getting western, about one second before the horse fell off the trail."

"Off *that* trail?"

Dave nodded. "It bounced a couple of times on the way down, but once it hit the water it started swimming. Straight out to sea. Till it sank anyway. We knew we'd seen the last of that horse, but all of a sudden, up it blows, like some kind of submarine. Decided it'd had enough of swimming. Turned straight back for shore." Dave looked at me. "It's for sale now, if you're looking."

"I'll keep that in mind," I said, then asked about Kelly, details of whom seemed oddly scarce.

"In the hospital. Foot surgery. Or ankle. Metal pins. Screws. Plates. I'm not sure what all."

"Could've been worse," Gags said.

"Oh, yeah," Dave agreed. "Way worse." He pushed the throttle forward, off to meet my horse.

Gibson Reservoir, Montana
May 2004

As Dave pounded through the chop, we neared the end of the lake, a group of men and horses flashing in and out of sight between the silvery-green trunks of a stand of flooded aspen. Behind the trees rose a broken rocky point and, along its right, a long, lushly green hill, a muddy brown slash of trail winding up its face. Nolan would be thinking elves, dwarves, the path to Mordor. Aidan would be all about the horses, Legolas's full-gallop mounting technique.

Dave nudged the boat into the bank, and I hopped out and pulled us up. Tom, the warden and packer who'd bring the eggs and me the last fifteen miles into the wilderness, pointed out that we were late. Hours late. I wanted to let him know that I'd been ready, but it didn't seem the cowboy way. And Tom didn't have time for it anyway. He'd called once, telling me to make my packs sixty pounds each, saying my waterproof river bags sounded acceptable. Now he slapped them down onto big squares of canvas, mantees, bundling them up, trussing them with a series of hitches, calling for mules by name. I stood out of the way and tried to be, if not helpful, at least observant.

Pete was the only mule I connected with a name, jumping forward when Tom called for him, then quietly stepping back when someone led over a black, oddly skinny, long-legged beast that looked at least as much moose as mule. Only three years old, and on his first pack trip, he was the one Tom picked to carry my bags—not the grayling eggs, anything essential.

Tom tugged at the pack saddle, grabbing its two steel arches, rocking it. Not quite satisfied, he crouched down to tighten the cinch strap behind the mule's front legs, then turned and reached under to adjust the belly strap.

The kick, in the first half of an instant, seemed like nothing much, just a lifted leg, a bunching of muscles, a hoof raised at some minor irritant. Flies maybe. Just that little flash of iron shoe. The next half an instant was too quick for any eye to trace, but nothing seemed minor anymore. There was the sound, that solid home-run crack, the drop of a melon, and then there was Tom, sailing through the air, legs spread-eagled, arms too. He twirled, pancake flat, facedown toward the grass and the pinecones, at least a revolution, but again, too fast to really quite catch. Then he was down, struggling back up to his knees, his forearms, in some sort of fighting instinct, weaving, rocking, a thick rope of blood drooling from mouth to ground. Pete, the mule, stood quiet, as if nothing at all had happened, the pack saddle still on his back, the straps still not quite tight enough.

I'd been watching Tom's every move, hoping to maybe learn something—what I knew about horses would rattle in a peapod—and I was the only one who saw the kick. But heads turned at that sickening, fatal sound, as I was already dropping to a knee beside Tom, putting an arm over his shoulders to keep him from dropping onto his side. He moaned a low, repetitive, "Whoa, whoa, whoa." The blood came not just from his mouth, but from his chin, his nose, and I couldn't stop a glance to his ear, fearing more blood there, the clear cranial fluid I'd seen in car-crash victims, but so far, nothing. The sound of the hit still shivered. I couldn't believe he was conscious. Even alive.

His temple was slightly purpled, already swelling, and, reaching to touch, I feared the give and grate of loose bone, another thing familiar from accidents, but nothing shifted, nothing sponged down. His head, somehow, felt whole, intact, but he didn't wince at the touch, or even look up. "Tom," I said. "Tom?" The others gathered around, quiet "holy shits," and "oh my Gods" encircling us.

Tom stopped rocking, slowly lifted his head. He put it back down and reached into his pocket for a kerchief. He began dabbing it against his face, his mouth. He held it out, looking at his blood. He wasn't yet spitting out teeth.

He pushed himself up from his elbows to his hands, dropping back to his haunches.

"Easy," I said. "Easy does it, Tom."

The others echoed, "Go easy now." "You okay?" "Don't try getting up just yet."

He wiped away enough blood that we could see a gash on his chin, a split and swollen lip. He let me look in his mouth. Another long gash inside his cheek. But all his teeth still there, still whole. I felt his head again. Still solid.

"Any idea what day it is, Tom?" I asked.

Somehow, he smiled. "Thursday."

"Good," I said, "good. How about the year?"

He thought for a bit. "2004."

"You're a genius," I said.

He wanted to stand, and we helped him to his feet. We let go, but stood close. All I could guess was that the hoof had missed the skull, maybe glanced off his chin, that it had been the rear of the leg that connected with Tom's head. At least a little hair and meat for padding.

A stunned and whispery crowd, we kept asking, "You okay?"

Tom wiped again at the blood and said, "Could've been worse."

He walked a few small circles, gradually stretching his steps, testing his balance. We walked with him, ready to catch. Someone handed him his hat and he looked a little more whole without his hair poking in every direction. Somebody else dug out some Advil.

He rubbed at his eyes. "Vision's a little fuzzy yet."

Taking one more get-his-feet-under-him lap, Tom finally stopped, facing his mule. "Okay Pete, you son of a bitch. Let's try that again."

He leaned against the mule's side, pushing him where he wanted him. This time, reaching for the belly band, he kept his head toward Pete's head, not his rear. He tightened the strap a single notch. "My fault," he said. "Too much of a hurry. Went at it backwards."

He leaned over and hefted one of my manteed dry bags. I jumped to take the weight, but he grunted that it was easier if he did it himself, that getting the packs up onto the stock was really a one-man job.

Before I knew it, or was even close to ready for it, there was nothing left to do but go. Everyone stood around, sneaking peeks Tom's way. Nobody said much, nothing about swelling inside his skull, pressure building on his brain. I didn't think riding a full day into the wilderness was the smartest path to follow, but Tom only said, "No. No. I'm fine. Got my bell rung a little. That's all."

"Maybe we could have lunch," I said. "Wait a little bit first." Dave had told me that he and Tom would handle lunch and dinner the first day. A month's worth of food in the manteed loads, I didn't have any lunch.

"We're already late," Tom said. "We got to get these eggs in. Lee's waiting for us at Biggs. We've got a long day ahead of us." He patted one of the horses on the rump. "This is Gus, my daughter's horse. You'll be riding him."

He waited until I tugged myself up into the saddle, where I sat clutching the reins as if astride a keg of dynamite, fuse smoking.

Tom stepped up into the saddle of his horse. "Ready?" he asked.

"Are you?"

He nodded and turned his horse out of the trees. "You go ahead and I'll follow along with the string."

Clutching the saddle horn, I touched Gus's side with my heels, awaiting detonation. But Gus only stepped slowly forward, passing Tom, who had his head turned, spitting blood into the bushes, and lined himself into the trail like he'd been doing it all his life, like I was about as necessary as any of the packs we'd strapped onto Pete's back.

The other guys, their feet firmly on ground, called out good-byes and good lucks. Gags caught my eye and mouthed, *They're big, they're dumb, and sooner or later . . .*

I'd been past the point of no return for weeks, but now there was no denying it.

Lake Mead, Nevada
June 1978

This and Indian Creek weren't exactly the only times I'd jumped into things with no preparation or stepped blindly into things that could go so wrong so fast. Following Rader's urging to get into the Park Service any way I could, start anywhere, I sat in my dorm room and matched my skill set up against the National Park Service application. I was qualified for, well, nothing. At all. Until I spotted the opening for a lifeguard. In Lake Mead, Nevada. I'd never been anywhere near the southwest in my life. Had never harbored any desire to see Las Vegas. Could not really imagine what a gigantic lake in the desert would even look like. But I could swim. And I'd lifeguarded at pools for most of my working life—the last four years. So I Greyhounded down to Vegas, got picked up by my boss and driven out to the desert, the little cluster of park housing, sun-scorched two-bedroom units behind dead lawns, faded cottonwood trees.

I met my roommates, the other newbs, a kid from Connecticut, another from LA, and the next morning we met the rest of the crew at the lifeguard station, an ancient travel trailer, its paint bleached toward bare aluminum. Tanned darker than walnut, the vets grinned as we took in the beach: a stretch of graded, broken desert rock, too sharp to walk on barefoot, a flooded road disappearing into the water. "You'll get the tan," the boss assured us, kicking off a hardly laced running shoe, showing off the cavelike pallor of his foot.

That first week, before the real summer crowds started to show up, we ran drills, practiced leaping from the towers, shifting over, covering the water, got the hang of sprinting into the lake, unfurling our rescue tubes, kicking off our shoes just after our dive, so our feet wouldn't shred on the rocks before we started to swim.

A few mornings in, we were in the middle of one of our first sets of drills, only a handful of real swimmers in the water, one of our guards out there imitating a drowner. But she was in front of the tower one down the beach from mine, so while that guard leapt into the water and stroked out, snapped her into her rescue tube, towed her back to shore, my job was just to sprint to a point halfway between each tower, watching her water and mine. Over and over again.

On my way back to my tower, catching my breath, the day still early enough to keep the thermometer below one hundred, I heard the calls from the water, thought, *Man, at least let me get back to my tower,* but I turned, scanned the slight waves, just as I'd been trained.

I stopped, looked, looked again. If I'd been a dog, my head would have tipped to the side, that quizzical glance. Three men struggled out there, over their heads, shouting nothing intelligible. One managed a quick arm jerk of a wave. I didn't recognize any of them, none of the new faces I was learning from training. I pulled the strap from around my rescue tube, slipped it over my head, across my shoulder, still waiting for the punch line. My radio sat up in my tower, where I'd been told to leave it for the drills. I glanced both ways down the beach, the rest of the crew busy setting up for the next drill, no one even facing my way.

At last, barely guessing that this could truly be real (in my four years of pool lifeguarding, I'd had exactly zero rescues), I took off for the water, felt it pull at my feet, my ridiculous shoes, then my knees, thighs, and I dove, throwing the tube out to drag in my wake, kicked off my shoes. Head up, I stroked Tarzan-style out toward the men, who, as I got closer, I saw were huge Hispanic guys, still wearing their T-shirts. I pulled back, just out of reach, shoved the rescue tube toward them, shouted for the outside two, who seemed to be holding up the middle one, to snap him into it.

But they were beyond that, could only stare, eyes huge, just managing to keep their mouths above water. The center guy's face dipped into the water, didn't jerk back. Throwing out the rules, I came within their reach, pushed the tube beneath the armpits of the center guy, clipped him in, rolled him onto his back, grabbed each of the other guys under their enormous arms, gave them some idea of support, told them to hold onto the rescue tube too, started frog kicking toward shore, on my back, head up, watching them, expecting at any second a wave of lifeguards to break over us.

But I reached the shallows, stood, hobbled over the broken rock, still dragging the most exhausted until he started bumping bottom. The two who could walk made it to dry rock and collapsed, chests heaving, arms hooked over their knees, hands hanging heavy, hair straggling before their eyes. "Man," one gasped. "How come you just watch us? How come you don't come?"

I had no answer, and then the storm of guards did wash over us, took the last guy out of my tube, out of my hands, lay him down, watched over him. My boss turned to me, grinned. "Jesus, a triple. Way to start big."

The guy who'd really saved his friend stared at me through his hair. "How come you wait?"

I didn't say: Because I had no idea. Because I couldn't believe my own eyes. Because I never expected anything like this to actually happen. We were just practicing, pretending. Playing.

That evening, back up at the houses, I was the guy with the triple. Holy shit, a triple.

For the first year ever, no one died on Boulder Beach. Nor did anyone drown the next year. Or the year after that. I pulled dozens and dozens of desperate, drowning men and women and children from those blue waters in the desert: out too far, got too tired, drank too much, just not paying attention. I did CPR, successfully, on the first half dozen or so people I ever tried it on. Bringing them back from the dead. Afterward, the adrenaline seeping away, we'd joke about it, going all Frankenstein, *It's ALIVE!*

The supervisor by my second year, I learned to live for that adrenaline rush, that feeling that everything, people's very lives, depended upon me. And the drowners really did come back easily, no trauma, no broken bones, torn vessels, burst organs. Working the car wrecks, a whole different game.

Still, it remained a game. Keep the streak alive. Don't let anybody die.

Away from the beach, that treacherous game, I walked out into the desert behind my house, hiked canyons, toyed with sidewinders, chased after javelinas, found the small local herd of desert bighorns. More often, though, I fled for higher country, something resembling the north. I trekked up the Virgin River in Zion, holding my pack over my head. Scrambled over those odd white domes of rock until I reached the plateau, camped out in actual grass, under actual trees, ponderosa and aspen, dreams of Montana. I roasted for entire summers, months wearing little beyond the board shorts, barely glancing to the endless succession of scorched blue skies holding no mystery. And every fall, I raced back up north and reveled at the first night out, having to pull on a wool shirt. The scratch of wool. Like heaven.

But, in the end, it is true, we all have to die, not everyone can be saved every time, and the summer after I graduated from college, wildlife biology degree in hand, somebody finally did die on Boulder Beach, right in front of a tower. The radio call went out, the guard hit the water, the guard from the next tower moved over, everything like clockwork. Driving the truck, I raced in from the other end of the beach. The guard found him, lifted him off the bottom, up to the air, struggled with holding him there, and I pulled him away from her. Fist locked in his hair, I swam him to shore, dragged him over the rocks, did CPR, got him started again. Just a kid. A teenage boy. The ambulance raced him up to Boulder City, where he lived another day or so. I tried, telling only myself, that we'd gotten him going, that he hadn't died on my watch, but even I couldn't hide behind such finely split hairs.

Bob Marshall Wilderness, Montana
May 2004

We hadn't reached the top of the hill before Tom stopped to rearrange loads. Behind us, the lake, spotted with shifting glints of sparkling green as gaps opened through the clouds, lay still tantalizing in sight. Tom handed me the lead rope, told me to hold the stock. I wondered what I was supposed to do if they decided to go anywhere. But Tom finished before the horses could gather their wits, and we rode another few hundred yards, to the crest of the hill, the start of the trees. Tom told me to find one to tie off to, that he had to really adjust the loads. Two stops in fifteen minutes. And we were in a hurry.

Then Tom was up again, and a few seconds later, so was I, just remembering to untie Gus before clambering aboard. We plodded on, the trail going dark and cold, closed in by heavy timber, the soft pocks of the hooves in the dirt and needles, the creaks and knocks of the saddles and packs. The lake disappeared, only Lee, waiting for his grayling eggs, out there ahead of us.

The rhythm of Gus's gate, the long morning, lulled me into something approaching a doze until, behind me, Tom muttered, "Pete, you son of a bitch." I snapped around, but he was talking to his mule. I tried to sit straighter though, more alert, and a few miles later we dropped off the hill, into a break in the trees, and the North Fork stretched below us, wild looking, a series of drops, whitewater chutes I couldn't help but scan for floating routes.

Behind me, Tom muttered, "Whoa, whoa," not sounding all that unlike he had seconds after the kick.

I turned to see what now.

Tom swiveled in his saddle, searching left, right. "Oh, boy," he said. "Uh-oh."

"You okay?" I asked, wondering how many times he'd listen to that without directing a "son of a bitch" my way.

"I don't know," he answered. "I think we might have taken the wrong trail."

Back home I'd studied the map long enough to know that we only had to follow the river up to the pack bridge, about fifteen miles, then cross the river and up a mile or two to the cabin at Gates Park. At least I thought I had. "You sure?" I asked. This was his backyard, not mine.

"I don't recognize a thing here," Tom said. "Nothing at all." One of the mules behind him shied sideways, a clatter of hooves on rock, rearing heads, ropes springing taut. Without a glance back, Tom ripped at the lead. "Pete, you son of a bitch!"

The mules settled down, and I asked, "Don't we just follow the river? Doesn't the trail?"

Tom nodded, studying the lay of the land. "I don't know. This just doesn't look right."

"You want to go back? To that little fork? Or just keep going awhile, see if anything seems right?"

Tom turned around. "I don't know."

At last, he shook his head. "We might be backtracking later, but . . ." He nudged his horse forward, shaking his head. "I don't know."

It wasn't until we reached the sign-in box at the wilderness boundary that Tom became convinced we were on the right trail. Then his confusion seemed the oddest thing that had ever happened to him. "I can't believe I got turned around like that. I've been in here, on this trail, too many times to count."

"Probably not kicked in the head every time out."

"No, you got a point there."

After the boundary, the ride opened into grassland, mountains rising up on our right, the slope of grass heading down to the river, not always visible on our left, and beyond that, more mountains, more serious, snow-capped and jagged. I pointed out a line of bighorns threaded along a black cliff face. Tom said, "Sheep Ridge," which seemed promising, if he was right.

Elk stood in groups everywhere, ragged and shaggy in their shedding winter coats, doing little more than raising their heads at our passing, and Tom said he thought we might still have a chance of meeting Lee at the agreed-upon time, one o'clock.

We rode on. And on. Eventually, Tom said, "I read your book."

"Yeah, didn't have any idea what I was doing then either."

"I know," he said. "I read it." He rode ahead, his voice hard to make out unless he turned toward me. "And now I'm bringing that moose-poaching son of a bitch into my wilderness and dropping him off for a month alone."

I tried to keep my smile going. "I promise I'll leave your moose alone."

"Damn well better." He tried to smile, too.

At one o'clock, me twitching in the saddle, sore pretty much all over, eyes peeled for this Lee guy, Tom guessed we'd be closer to an hour late. Then an hour and a half. Half an hour after that, the saddle irritating places I hadn't known I'd had, we dropped down a long, green slope to the biggest creek yet, clear water tumbling over a wide bed of whitened, rounded rock. Biggs Creek, the first of the incubator sites.

Lee, napping in the sun, stood up groggily, smiling. I staggered down off of Gus. "How's that feel?" he asked. "Being on the ground again?"

"Pretty okay," I admitted. And it was all pretty okay. The smell of sun-heated pine filled the air, a scent, it seemed, I'd been too long away from. I took a few test steps, my legs like posts, watched my boots sink into the duff, toed the stiff, waxy leaves of Oregon grape. Lee stood staring at Tom as he tied off the horses and mules. When Tom turned to us, his bruised and split face on full display, his bloodied shirt, he had to tell the story, a version truncated by embarrassment as he unloaded the egg coolers, set them down beside the creek. "Too much rushing," he said, "not enough thinking."

Lee gave me a look and waved for me to follow him to the small spring where he'd set up the incubators. He wore hip boots. In Pete's carefully wrapped and balanced bundles, I had my own hip boots, and a pair of knee-high gum boots, but I wasn't about to ask Tom to unpack them just so I wouldn't get my feet wet.

I dropped into the sucking muck and tromped behind Lee to the three black five-gallon buckets standing in six inches of clear, flowing water, the kind of buckets I used for raft bailers. White PVC pipe fed into them from a pool up-stream, held behind a dam like all the ones the boys and I had built—rocks and sticks, mud and leaves. On the downstream side of each bucket, just below the rim, an inch of white pipe stuck out, water pouring from it back into the creek. The water, after cleaning away the mud covering my leather boots, drained into my socks.

"The last few years we tried stocking the river with fin-gerlings," Lee explained. "But they just washed down to the reservoir, and we don't need another adfluvial population. We need fluvial, so we're hoping having them hatch here will help hold them in the river."

Twenty years earlier, in the Tetons, I'd caught scads of adfluvial (lake dwelling) grayling in a remote lake where they'd been introduced in the fifties and then forgotten. A beautiful fish spattered with neon spots, they sport a dorsal fin like a fan, something more at home in the high seas with the marlin and sailfish. Nothing quite yet imaginable in the masses of spotted pink BBs in the coolers. Native to the Arctic, two small populations of grayling were left behind by the last ice age: one in Michigan, now extinct, and the other in the high valley of Montana's Big Hole River. I'd caught a few of those too, but they were threatened now: warming, drought, irrigation. "Maybe just the species' time," Lee said. "But we're hoping that with a second or third population, their chances for survival will be a little better."

Stooping over, he sloshed his hands inside a bucket until he pulled up a plastic mesh basket full of gravel. "Okay," he said. "This is the basic system. The water comes in from below, up through the gravel, over the eggs, and out the pipe at the top. Hopefully, the water carries the silt out the top, instead of letting it bury the eggs."

He dropped the gravel basket back down and reached to shore for a bag full of black plastic pieces. About an inch and a half long, they looked like miniatures of the cut-in-half, inside-out car tires used on playgrounds—little plastic arches pierced with a regular interval of holes. "These are biosaddles," Lee said. "We use them instead of, well, any other junk we'd throw in." The holes, he explained, were big enough for the eggs to sift through. "And, hopefully, when the time comes, for the fry to wriggle out on their way to bigger things." He dumped handfuls into the bucket, atop the gravel basket. "Gives them some cover and takes a lot of the silt load and, because of the holes, allows more water flow than plain old rocks. And maybe, because they're so lightweight, you can dig through them to check on progress without smashing as many eggs as you would otherwise."

He dropped the last of the saddles in over the gravel, four or five inches' worth. "That's it. Now we put the eggs in, and they sit down in all that until they hatch and swim out."

He poured more saddles into the other buckets, then, in the last, dropped in a white plastic mesh basket, a few inches square. "We'll leave some eggs in this, above the saddles, so you'll be able to see how they're progressing without digging through the saddles to look at them. The less disturbance, the better."

"Okay," I said.

"Silt is your main concern, and making sure they've got enough water, and, once they hatch and start swimming out, making sure they've got a clear shot downstream to the river."

Just upstream of each bucket, a red valve handle stuck up from the feeder pipe. "Use this to control the flow. You want the water just below the rim, without actually flowing over the top. You may or may not have to adjust them at all. Depends on the stream flow, how hot and dry it gets, how much rain."

Passing two more incubators on the way, we slogged upstream to the dam. At the bottom of the pool, each pipe was capped with a half-gallon milk bottle, plastic mesh cut into two sides. The intake filter. "Check these every day, and clean them when they need it. You'd turn off the water downstream first, of course, so you don't send a load of silt into the incubator."

"Of course."

"That's about all I can think to tell you. There are five

incubators here, then five up river, above the cabin, at Spruce Creek."

"Didn't want to put all your eggs in one basket," I said.

He'd heard that one before. "Water can dry up, silt load can suffocate the eggs. Bears. Who knows? So we spread them out as much as we could."

"Bears?"

Lee shrugged. "We've never done this in grizzly country. The eggs don't smell much. To me anyway. But I suppose to a bear they could be big buckets of caviar. You should be careful coming in to check on them."

I looked down at the buckets, then into the snarls of brush, the thickets of trees blocking even the sun. "So what am I supposed to do about the silt, if it gets heavy?"

"Ah, right." He bent over a bucket and swirled his fingers around in the water, creating a mini-whirlpool. "That should get up light silt, lift it enough to send it out the exit pipe." He reached deeper, found the two string loops attached to the gravel basket. "If it gets heavier, lift these," he said. "About an inch or two, and then let the basket fall. That'll stir up some of the silt, dislodge it, and the water flow will send it up. Then finger swirl to suck it out the exit. That's the theory anyway."

Tom, holding an egg cooler at the lip of the cut, asked, "Ready for these?"

We scrambled to help. Lee took the water temperature inside the coolers. Fifty degrees. "The water here's forty-two," he said. "Shouldn't shock them too bad. I hope." He turned to me with a shrug. "That's another thing you need to do. I've got a log book. Water temperature, air temperature, what the weather's like. Anything about the eggs: how they look, what changes in them, what silting activity you have, that kind of thing."

"If a grizzly's sitting in the stream, a bucket under each arm, lapping them up?"

"That'd be worth mentioning."

"If I live to tell about it."

"After all those eggs, he should be full."

"They sent in three coolers," Tom said, still annoyed about having to evenly pack an odd number. "So, we got a cooler and a half to split between each site."

"A cooler and a half divided by five incubators," Lee mumbled, pouring water out of the first cooler, leaving the eggs an undisturbed mass near the bottom.

"Wow," Lee said, "look at them. They're really far along."

"Active," I said. Occasionally, if you looked hard enough, you could see one roll a little, kind of vibrate for an instant.

Lee nodded. "Active as hell. I don't think you'll be in here a month. These things could be hatching out in days. You might be out of here in a week, week and a half."

After all this? "Not if I don't tell you they're gone," I said, but I couldn't quite keep a certain leap from my heart, the thought of being back with the boys so soon.

Even Tom laughed a little. "Yeah, you'd have to let us know."

Without further ceremony, Lee tipped the cooler over the first bucket, letting about a third of the eggs drop in.

He'd turned the water off, so the eggs wouldn't flush out the exit pipe, and they drifted down, disappearing among the biosaddles.

The whole time he worked, he kept his shadow over the eggs. "That's another thing. They're very light sensitive. Direct sunlight screws the DNA, so, when you open the incubators, make sure you shade them. Until they've hatched. Once they've hatched, you take the lids off, but you have to find some rocks or logs or something to give partial shade until they adjust to the sunlight."

He reached around the bucket and gave the red faucet handle several turns, getting the water level just right. Then he divvied the last of the cooler among the other two buckets, leaving about a hundred eggs in the little white basket—my observation guinea pigs. A few of those eggs, instead of pink and eyed, were a dull, opaque white. "Those are dead," Lee said. "Try picking them out if you can without too much disturbance." He demonstrated, using the tip of a spoon, but several live eggs swirled up out of the basket, where they sank down among the biosaddles.

"Well, never mind. Leave them unless they start growing fungus. They'll look hairy. Then get them out right away. The fungus spreads fast and kills the eggs it infects."

Leave the dead eggs, but not the hairy dead eggs. Turn the water off before cleaning the intakes. Never forget to turn the water back on. Water level up to, but not over, the rim. Lift and drop for heavy silt, finger swirl for light. No sunlight, until they've hatched. Then moderate sunlight, before full. Lids on the buckets until they've hatched, then off.

Clear a channel for the fry. Record temperatures. Watch out for bears.

As if he could hear me thinking, Lee said, "I've got it all written down up at the cabin. We'll go over it again up there."

Looking pinched and gray, Tom repacked the coolers and asked if I was ready to go. Barely keeping myself from asking if he was okay, I offered some of the Advil I'd pocketed for the ride. I was sore enough already to toss back a few, but Tom took them all. I untied Gus, walked him around. I'd had time to stiffen up.

I asked Lee if he wanted to ride the last little bit, but he only grinned. "I'll get my fill tomorrow on the ride out. Believe me." He splashed across the river, hiking up the steep cut on the other side.

I climbed on board and shifted in the saddle, trying to find some comfortable spot. How on earth would the boys have endured this? Walking? Riding on my lap?

Behind me, Tom said, "Anytime you're ready."

10

Lake Mead, Nevada
1980

The one rescue at Lake Mead that definitely did not count as a death on the beach came in first as a phone call to 911, which was then routed through to our park headquarters in Boulder City, then through radio, down to me at the beach. A man at the marina had called in a possible drowning in progress along the causeway, a jutting line of riprap boulders built out into the lake as a breakwater for the marina. Taking Tim, the guard on break, I started for the boat, looking across the water to the causeway. About three quarters of a mile away, it stretched nearly half a mile long. I asked for a more precise location and was told they had none. A man, they said, would wave me down.

We swam to the boat, a seventeen-foot, flat-bottomed Boston Whaler with a jet, no prop to chop through the swimmers. I fired it up, and we hammered full throttle toward the rock jetty. And, true enough, as we got closer, out near the end we could make out a man in a white T-shirt, waving both hands over his head.

I cut the throttle, drifting us in, Tim reaching out front to keep us from bashing the rocks. Already things were hyperfocusing, the two girls with the man nothing more than shapes. The man himself hardly registered, shouting something in a language I couldn't understand, pointing down into the water, sobbing, shouting, pointing. I had my fins on, my mask, and I went over the side, the world going still and silent and green, silt covered rocks stretching down and away into darkness.

This far out, the jumble of boulders dove into water that may as well have been bottomless. I turned toward that blackness, kicking for it, the dead, gray rocks descending as steeply as I could dive.

At the limit of my dive, swimming along the rock wall, I caught the glimmer of her, still far below, the white of her T-shirt matched by the pallor of her legs, her arms. The green of the water, the gray of the silt. I kicked down. She stretched from the point of a rock, an outcrop, on her back, arms adrift to her sides as she gazed toward the surface, only a foot or so from missing the rock completely, drifting down farther, out of sight and gone.

Already out of air, I turned for the surface, knowing I'd never reach her at the end of this dive. I kicked hard, dolphin kicks, the fins driving me up. The surface shifted and sparkled, almost blinding after looking into the deep.

I broke through, sucking in air. Tim stood on shore, holding the boat. "Found her," I said. "She's deep."

I took one more gulp and threw myself back down, flipping my legs into the air, the pull of gravity giving that much more of a start.

I kicked as hard down as I had up. I'd never been anywhere near this deep before, and by the time I reached out, caught a swirl of her waving mermaid's hair, I was already fighting the urge to breathe, that odd, choked-throat gulping, the body struggling with itself to breathe / not breathe. I turned with her, pushed off her rock, driving for the surface, for the air, the light above.

My head burned, throbbed. I hummed, or moaned, something, kicking, kicking, the whole dolphin sweep disintegrating, barely jerks. I wondered about letting go, about not making it to the sky, and then there was Tim—just appeared, where had he come from?—tugging her away from me, freeing me from her dead weight, and I broke the surface, the stars of the light on the water indistinguishable from the pops and flashes of the lack of oxygen. I leaned back, floating for a moment, gasping. Tim pulled the girl onto the rocks. The man, I think, howled. I rolled over, stroked the last yards to the rocks. We carried her to the flat top of the causeway, picking our way up the boulders. I took the chest, counting out the downward strokes, the drive against her heart. Every fifth pump, Tim pinched shut her nose, sealed her lips with his, blew his air into her lungs.

Soon, a siren. An ambulance creeping down the crushed rock path atop the causeway. I went into the back with her, staying on the chest, telling Tim to take the boat back, start the breakdown of the towers at the regular time, do the routine. The ambulance crewman took over the breaths, intubated her, squeezed air in with the Ambu bag rather than going mouth to mouth.

There was little doubt, but we continued to the hospital; let the doctors make that call. I wondered how long she'd been lying snagged on that rock, caught up short in her fading away toward the bottom.

I went in with her through the emergency doors, stood back when the pros took over. Needles and paddles and machines. The doctor didn't waste much time. Pupils dilated, unreactive. A few more tests.

The adrenaline in full retreat, I saw that she was thin. Maybe fifteen. Maybe on the edge of pretty. Asian. I tried to picture the man, if I'd seen that he was Asian, wondered if he was. The other girls. Younger, I thought. Maybe. Sisters?

I shivered, standing in my lifeguard shorts in the air-conditioning.

The doctor called it. Noted the time.

I walked out, still shivering, down the cold halls, the waxed and polished linoleum clammy against my naked feet. My ears hurt, pressure popped, like when driving over a mountain pass, or lifting off in a plane, off to somewhere else, somewhere far enough away you needed to fly. I wondered how I'd get back down to the lake. What time it was. If Tim had closed the beach for the day. If it was over yet.

And then someone stopped me, grabbing my shoulder. Or, really, just touching it. I turned, and there was the man from the causeway, tears on his face, bowing to me, reaching for my hand, saying, I think, "Thank you," over and over.

I nodded back, having no idea what to say. His

daughter was dead. I had brought back nothing but an empty shell. I took his hand, and he bowed again and turned away to go back to her. The back of his T-shirt was missing. His thin back, the trail of his spine a fault line splitting the low ranges of his shoulder blades, was scratched red, clawed and bleeding, and I saw, hours before the investigating ranger would show me his report, this man fishing on the causeway with his daughters, this clan of nonswimmers, saw how, in the heat, the girls had waded out onto the knee-deep water over the first rocks, the step one took beyond the edge of that rock, how she suddenly found nothing beneath her feet, started to thrash against the water, a medium she had no greater ability to float in than air, saw a sister reach for her and find the same nothing, the father leaping in, his girls climbing over him to the air, how he'd scrambled for purchase, slipped, the three of them, or maybe all four now, suspended, sinking, bobbing, heads tilting back toward the sky, the father turning, shoving one of the girls toward the rocks, whichever one he could reach, another, the last, the oldest, behind him, climbing him, pushing him under, sinking him, the one who struggled only to stay on him, on top of him, in the air, the one he had to fight off to reach a rock with his feet, turn for to pull in after him, only to find open, empty water, stretching out, stretching down, away from him, forever. I saw him count his other daughters, demand they stay still, not move, as he ran the half mile to the marina, barefoot over the rocks, begged for a phone, for help, ran back out while we fired up the boat and bounced across the lake top toward the desperate little figure, already far too late, his white T-shirt, arms waving above his head, calling out in his own language, *I'm here. We're here. Help us. Please. Save us.*

I went back to Missoula, staying with friends still in school. I filled out the paperwork for the Park Service's seasonal law enforcement school, the only path up out of the desert, out of my lifeguard shorts, away from Lake Mead. In November I drove out to Santa Rosa, California, spent the next couple of months living in a cell in a closed youth-detention center, learning to be a ranger with a gun.

Then back to Missoula, filling out my applications for real ranger jobs, sending them out to Yellowstone and Grand Teton, mountains in the north, out of the desert, places I actually wanted to be, the Tetons still the Shangri-la from that family vacation ten years before, no longer quite half my life ago.

My boss from Lake Mead called, wondering. I told him no, I couldn't; I was done. He wanted to know where he could send his recommendation.

My first offer came from a ranger in Yellowstone, wanting to hire me for the road patrol, driving a cruiser, working traffic, speeding tickets, car wrecks, shattered bodies. Trying to sound as enthusiastic as I could, I put him off, made up some excuse, a week to consider, clinging to the hope of the Tetons. And, just as time ran out, I got a letter from the sub-district supervisor in charge of the river patrol. It promised nothing, just asked me to fill out a further application specifying all my river-running experience—the River Screen Out.

The job, it seemed, was to spend all day, every day, floating the Snake alone, looking for rescue work, checking fishing licenses maybe. I could hardly breathe, but as I scanned through the form, it looked like a joke, every single question designed as if to specifically highlight my complete lack of experience.

So I made myself up.

That one trip I sat as a passenger on a tourist boat became seasons. A veteran boatman I. A river runner extraordinaire. A veritable Neptune. I could, I figured, learn on the job.

The subdistrict ranger, it turned out, used to work with a ranger at Lake Mead. My next-door neighbor. The guy who'd thought to drive up to the hospital that evening and give me a lift back down to the lake. They talked. I got hired.

My first official duty in Grand Teton National Park, the moment I first walked through the door of the old homesteader's log cabin I was to live in, was to dash straight back out, following my new roommate, Pancoast, a square-jawed, rosy-cheeked, flaxen-haired all-American boy. I hopped into the pickup beside him, and he tore off as if the fate of the free world hung in the balance. I belted in, asking what was the emergency. He glanced over, told me we had to bring back enough snow to keep the keg cold for that night's season-opening bash. I smiled, said okay.

The next morning the whole river crew met at the river for a shakedown cruise, all of us a bit worse for wear. The snow drove down sideways, and we stood huddled, nobody really wanting to move. Smiling, so far from the desert, I started out, but really had no idea how to rig the raft. They watched me fumble, glancing at each other, back to me.

I grinned, shrugged, fessed up. They howled. Loved it. They moved to help, and we got the boat into the water in seconds, clambered aboard, shoved off, and as we drifted downriver, regaling ourselves with stories from the night before, they began to teach me the ways of the river, ferry angles, the double-oar turn. To the west, always, the Tetons jutted into the sky, edging the world. Snow, mountains, all this roaring water. It was almost as if the desert, that penned-up lake of a river and everything that sank into it, had never existed.

The next morning, the boss called us all into the little office and gave us a shakedown talk, letting us know his plans for the season, one that wandered into a ramble, turning more and more paranoid every minute, warning us never to use the word "hazard" on our river-information handouts, how the lawyers would be all over that, how we'd be held *liable,* a word he used again and again as he got more worked up. Across the room, Pancoast caught my eye, gave a tiny shake of his head, and stuck his hand out, rolling his thumb over his fingers as if fidgeting with Captain Queeg's steel marbles. One person in a hundred, a thousand maybe, might have gotten the reference, but I saw Humphrey Bogart hunched over there, "But the strawberries, that's where I had them!" and, turning purple trying to hold in the laughter, knew I had a friend for life.

11

Bob Marshall Wilderness, Montana
May 2004

I'd thought at Biggs Creek that the ride was nearly over, the eggs, as I'd been told, only a mile or two from the cabin. But after we crossed the long, open, grassy stretch of Biggs Flat, scattering more elk, the grass gave out and we rode through miles of burned timber, nothing but charred black sticks jutting into the sky, victims of the huge '88 fires, burned over again in 2001. Gus, finally sensing the day's end, broke into a trot, and I shifted hopelessly in the saddle. Tom told me to haul him in. "That trot shakes hell out of the packs."

"Me too," I said, tightening the reins, a direction Gus obeyed for a few hundred yards before goosing it back up. Again and again.

The trail dropped down to the river, something we hadn't seen since before Biggs, to the pack bridge that led up the other side to Gates Park, my home, but we rode past, climbing back up onto a knifed bluff above the river, the views widening through the burn, then closed off completely in an area untouched by the second big burn in 2001, the twelve-foot-tall lodgepoles making it impossible to see more than a few feet. Then we were back into burn, edging the bluff above the river, and Tom pulled the train to a halt and pointed down to the river. "Spruce Creek," he said.

Even facing the steep tangle of charred, fallen trees, wondering how we'd haul the coolers down through it, I ached to get off my horse, to ask if we were there yet.

I set foot on the ground, my knees stiff and rubbery at the same time, my ass and back shot. Tom unleashed the coolers, and we poured all the eggs into one. Lee said he'd chopped a sort of path down to the incubators. While Tom stayed with the stock, we began the descent, three-point as often as not, and spent another hour loading the last of the eggs into the Spruce Creek buckets. Rather than any sort of a swamp, the creek here was steep and rocky, a free fall down the ridge, pooling here and there only to fall again. The buckets themselves were in the creek's short tail out before entering the river, and Lee said silt could be a real enemy here, a heavy rain roaring through this burned country bringing a cascade of topsoil and ash along with it.

Crawling back up the hill, we met Tom and the horses, and I again asked Lee if he wanted to ride, almost begged him, but he only smiled and set off afoot.

I walked around Gus, and Tom talked about different ways to come here, walking up the west side of the river, crossing at Ray Creek, coming back down, just to change things up.

I nodded and wrestled my way into the saddle, and as we started back the way we'd come, Tom rethought the Ray Creek trail. "A lot of bears back that way," he said. He thought awhile longer, then started into a story the Forest Service trail foreman had told him the previous summer.

The trail crew had been staying at Gates but had to follow their work up to a spike camp near Ray Creek. One of the crew members, reaching his days off, needed to get to town. A girlfriend. The foreman told him he couldn't spare him a horse and warned him not to be late coming back for work four days later. The kid hit the long trail afoot.

Four days later, after a hard time saying good-bye, wearing shorts and a day pack, he came tearing back, running stretches to make up time. Even so, by the pack bridge he was using a headlamp to see the trail. It was almost midnight by the time he reached Gates, but still he forged on, finally within striking distance of the spike camp.

"He was about halfway there," Tom said, waving into the thick stands of green trees around us, the dense patches of brush, "stuff like this, when, instead of the trail, his headlamp lit up a mountain of hair, a small pair of eyes."

He let that sink in. "He took one step backward, tripped, and rolled onto his stomach, the last thing he thought he'd ever do."

The bear jumped at him, his feet striking down just in front of his face, three-inch claws gleaming in the little circle of his headlamp. Huffing quick grunts, the bear bounced up and down in place, raising dust from the trail. Then it moved, walking around the kid, over him, its feet crushing his backpack against him. The hair of its legs brushed along the kid's bare legs. It lowered its nose to the back of his neck, snuffling, rubbing wetly back and forth.

Not able to guess how long the bear stayed on top of him, he could only say that it left "after a while," and he stayed right where he was, not daring to even lift his head, for what he figured was about fifteen minutes. All was silent, and black, except for that tiny circle of light in the trail in front of his face, where the claws had been.

Gathering himself, he stood to make a break for it.

He didn't get to his first step. The bear charged out of wherever he'd been watching, and knocked him flat. The whole process repeated itself, the bear walking over and around him, standing on him, snuffling his neck. Then, again, it walked away. He guessed that this time he waited two hours, alone on that black trail, and that when he did finally bolt, he never even stood up before getting his feet under him and going roadrunner.

"But when he reached the spike camp," Tom said, "it was empty. They'd moved upriver another few miles."

Tom shook his head. "Can you imagine? Come running in there, looking for everybody, anybody, and the whole place empty?"

He pushed the horses forward, across Headquarters Creek, the pack bridge in sight. "The next morning, the foreman rode back to the spike camp, thinking the kid might have made it to there but then couldn't guess where they'd gone."

He smiled, but couldn't quite laugh. "He found him in the cook tent, barricaded behind a complete ring of sleeping bags, empty candy wrappers scattered all around him. He'd just sat there the rest of the night, eating candy bars, hoping somebody would show up and tell him the grizzlies hadn't eaten everybody."

The next time he was out of the backcountry, the kid was debriefed by the bear specialists in Choteau, questioned in depth about the encounter. "Everybody yells grizzly every bear they see, so they tend not to believe you. They got this poor guy into an office and the biologist asks, 'It was night. Dark. How do you know it was a grizzly?'

"'It was a grizzly all right,' the kid says.

"'Did you get a chance to see its face? Its hump? Its claws?'

"'Goddamn right I saw its claws.'

"'How long were they?'

"The kid just jumps out of his chair, holding his hands about a foot and a half apart. 'This fucking long! At least! Okay? I got one helluva look at its claws!'"

Tom and I both smiled, but not at the kid's expense. We could picture ourselves in that patch of night, the one tiny circle of light, those glistening claws. I could picture it all too well.

We crossed the bridge, the horses clip-clopping over the timbers, me unable to keep from whispering, "Who's that tripping over my bridge!"—the Billy Goats Gruff I'd read a hundred times. We climbed through more burn, passed the waterfall of Gates Creek, a barrier Lee said kept the rainbows out, leaving the trout above one of the few remaining stocks of genetically pure westslope cutthroat. We entered more dark, green timber, the trail tight and muddy.

Finally the horses picked their way through a flooded, hoof-sucking patch of swampy grass, and there before us stood a sagging buck-rail fence, a gate. Civilization.

We crossed through the open gate, leaving it for Lee to close, and I saw a collapsing, windowless shack, and Tom said, "Home sweet home." I thought, for just an instant, *You've got to be kidding.* Dave had described the Gates Park cabin as the crown jewel of the Forest Service. This hulk?

Tom shifted in his saddle and smiled. This was one of the original homestead buildings, he told me. In another minute we cleared the trees, and the corrals and tack shed came into view and then the bunkhouse, dark logs behind the stark white line of a freshly peeled hitching rail. And, finally, the main cabin, more dark logs, cedar shingles stained green, a stove-pipe chimney, a roofed porch, heavy bear-proof shutters bolted over each window. Beyond the buildings stretched a mile of grass airstrip, abandoned since the wilderness designation in 1964, then a timbered rise back up into more mountains. A hundred or so elk grazed the airstrip, keeping the grass fairway tidy.

We tied up at the bunkhouse rail and Tom went straight to unpacking. I carried the packs over to the side of the bunkhouse, dropped them down on the grass, able to help at last. Leading the stock toward the corrals, Tom gave Lee and me cooking duty.

We wrestled the packs out of their mantees, loaded their contents into the back half of the bunkhouse: a dark storage room loaded with stacked bags of horse pellets, fire packs, bundles of rope, big, blocky water jugs for the fire lookouts. A platform of lashed-together lodgepole sticks hung from the ceiling: mouseproof food storage. I hung my loaded packs from the end rails of the platform, told Lee I'd help him with dinner. "I'll have time to unpack tomorrow," I said.

Grabbing what we needed, we stepped out of the murk of the windowless room into the bright evening, the sky deepening to azure, the scudding clouds reddening.

Instead of heading straight for the cabin, Lee led me toward the creek, to a food cache burrowed into the side of the hill like a hobbit hole. He ducked under the little awning roof and unlocked the massive half door. A gust of musty air surged out as he opened the door, shone a headlamp in. Above the faded lettering on the shelf edges—a system of order long ago abandoned for chaos—sprawled a rabble of canned fruit and vegetables, leaning towers of sardines and tuna, piles of repeat condiments, enough mayo and mustard to hold a barbecue for the state, a clutter of hams. Here and there a ruptured can stood covered with a fuzz of mold, like antlers in velvet, mouse turds scattered liberally through it all. A tube of plastic shrink wrap, its label its only contents, let me know that it had once been a summer sausage called Yard-O-Beef. The mice had chewed in one end and out the other, licking the plastic clean. Same for most of the bag of hamburger buns beside it, though there was a little green chip of one left behind. Not my mother's idea of a pantry.

I whispered, "Jesus," and Lee reached in for a couple

cans of corn. "Your stuff will stay sort of cool in here. Your cans mostly won't freeze. Dry stuff's okay in the bunkhouse, but you should try to keep most of your food in here."

He pushed the door shut, blasting out another shot of the cavernous earth reek, a dank mix of mold and dry dirt, tinged with staling food.

Before giving me his set of keys, Lee unlocked both doors of the main cabin, and together we undid the nuts on the inside walls and pushed the ten-inch bolts through the logs, then went back out to drop the shutters. With the windows unblocked, the cabin lit up, revealing a single metal bunk at the south window, a bunk-bed duo in front of the east. The last of the sun streamed low through the west window, spilling across the white wooden dining table, long enough, with its benches, to seat ten. On the north wall stood the wood-heating stove, a propane cook stove, a single faucet sink. Cold running water. The Ritz. Home sweet home.

It was past nine before Tom came back from letting the stock loose on the airstrip. Lee pulled T-bones from the grill, the pasta and corn from the stove. We could have fed ten, but I hadn't eaten a thing since a donut fourteen hours earlier, and though the wooden bench was hard on my long-saddled rear, I had no complaints.

Tom passed around the last of their beer supply, and I asked one last time how he was feeling. He sipped from his can, said, "Could have been worse."

Lee headed off to the bunkhouse, where he'd been sleeping all week, and Tom took the top bunk, and I the single at the south window. I carried one dry bag back from the bunkhouse, undid the straps, pulled out my sleeping bag and the pillow Aidan had given me: a stiff cutout in the shape of Batman's cowled head, ears and all, his grim face stitched in black and white, a thin slash of stern mouth.

Tom raised an eyebrow.

"My six-year-old," I said. "A strong believer in the protective power of superheroes."

His "Do I have to die?" phase, "Do you have to die?" wasn't even quite a year old. When I had to admit it was true, he asked if I'd live for twenty more years, the biggest number he could grab hold of. I assured him I'd do my best.

Tom nodded, and I asked if he was ready for the lantern. He was, and I turned the knob and slid into my sleeping bag as the glow faded. As I had camping as a kid, my father standing in the middle of the big canvas tent, his hand on the knob, my brothers and sisters lined out in thick, cottony sleeping bags, I listened to the dying hiss and watched the mantels glow orange, then red, dimmer and dimmer, until finally I wasn't sure if I was only watching an image lingering on my retina. But even that winked out, and I lay in the blackness, Tom's breathing already slow and steady. My head on Aidan's pillow, I turned toward the window, watched the moon rise over the trees, the mountains, lighting the meadow. Not even a year ago, we'd been walking the Highline trail in Glacier, the steep, skinny part, cliff on one side, abyss on the other, and he'd gotten spooked. I showed him how he was walking against the cliff, how I'd block his way over the drop, never let him fall. Eyes ready to tear, he shook his head. That wasn't the problem. Nearly trembling, he said, "But, Dad, what would I ever do if *you* fell?"

In Great Falls, the same moon sifted through the branches of the spruce at their bedroom window, my empty rocker between their beds. Ten thirty, they'd have been asleep for a couple of hours, something that for me, I knew, was still hours away.

12

Bob Marshall Wilderness, Montana
May 2004

When Tom's feet slapped the floor at five the next morning, I'd already been waiting an hour. I popped up as if out of a jack-in-the-box, struck a match to the lantern, another to the burner under the coffee, started a fire in the stove while Tom stuffed his arms into his jacket and said he'd wake Lee. "If the two of you get breakfast going, I'll gather the stock and saddle them. We'd like to get an early start." They didn't have the boat ride at the lake, but the whole distance on horseback, twenty-one, twenty-two miles. I couldn't wait to hand over the reins.

Tom stepped into the darkness, the rain loud in the few seconds the door was open, the wind gusting in.

The coffee was perking when Lee blew in, pushing the door shut on the weather. We set once again to cooking, and when we had the hash browns done, the pancakes, the sausage and bacon, I poked my head out to see if Tom was close. It was dawn, as light as it was going to get under the tree-scraping overcast. The stock stood tied before the tack shed, heads hung low. I called, and Tom shouted back, "Just let me know when you're ready."

I told him we were and Lee started cracking eggs, the whole dozen. We loaded our plates and reloaded them. I poured coffee, lots of it: thick enough to float a horseshoe—strong enough to melt it; hot and strong, just like my women—cold and bitter, just like yours. In tents and cabins, around stoves and fires, I'd heard them all.

Afterward, dazed, our silverware pushed onto empty plates, leftovers scattered across the table, we sipped at the dregs, blew out long breaths, looked out the window at the watery gray light, the trees dripping and dark. Tom used his arms to push up away from the table, said, "Well, might as well," and they left to finish readying the horses.

I laced up my new Gore-Tex boots and zipped tight my old Park Service North Face rain gear, still waterproof after twenty years. I threaded my Park Service .357 onto my belt and, on the left hip, my new can of bear spray. I crammed my size 12 hip boots into my day pack and threw it over my shoulder, ready as I'd get, like the boys on their first day of school.

The rain was light but steady, and Lee pulled on rain pants before stepping into the saddle. Holding the pack train's lead rope, Tom said they'd stop for me at Biggs, where Lee would give my final exam. I watched them start up the hill behind the cabin, the mules strung out behind. I waited until they were out of sight before shuttering the windows against the bears and setting out, slipping and sliding in the hoof-torn mud, breakfast lodged like a boulder in my belly, the rain pattering down, dripping off everything.

I caught the horses at the pack bridge, Tom adjusting his loads. He asked, "Did you see the bear tracks?"

I glanced behind me. "Nope."

"Horses probably blotted them out. Don't worry; you'll see plenty more."

"Black?" I asked, "or grizzly?"

"Grizzly. They seem to use that trail from Gates down to the river a lot."

Same trail I'd use every day. "That's great," I said.

We set off again, me losing ground uphill but seeming to have a horse's pace on the level, keeping them in sight all the way across the grassy two-mile stretch of Biggs Flat, until, an hour and a half after we'd set out, they dropped into the cut of the creek. The rain drove down, blurring my views, cutting them off completely less than half a mile in any direction.

At the top edge of the creek cut, I glimpsed the pack string lined along the far side of the creek, heads low in the rain. I slithered down after them, catching myself against trees now and then, the descent something of a glissade.

On my side of the creek, I sat down to pull on my hip boots for the crossing, the egg inspection. A few degrees too warm for snow, the rain kept on, the drops dangling from the edge of my hood, running back and forth with every dip of my head. I tugged at my sodden bootlaces, peeled off my squishy socks, wondered if Merrell had put the Gore-Tex in inside out.

The creek, high and murky, didn't quite roar but was

loud enough that when I stood, saw Tom on the other side, his leather chaps stained dark with rain, his lips moving, I had to cup a hand to my ear and shrug.

He yelled something, but I shook my head and started into the water, slogging over to him. Only knee deep, the creek shoved against my legs, the rounded rocks rolling out from under my feet, tumbling downstream.

I pulled out beside Tom and he said, "Was trying to tell you I found a tree downstream, one you can cross on without getting your feet wet."

"Okay," I said. "That's good to know."

As Tom balanced the packs, Lee gave me a last go through of egg procedures, handing me a Ziploc with a thermometer and spoon, logbook and pencils. My tool belt. Already five miles into his ride out, he had his riding boots on instead of his waders, so he stood at the bank, watching me go through the motions in the creek.

The grayling eggs in the observation basket stared up at me, one-eyed. Now and then one of them wiggled. "Not quite so active today," I said.

"It's colder," Lee answered. "That slows them down. Just not too much I hope." He pulled at his chin. "I don't know. The cold could stop them for a couple of weeks. A month. Forever." He shrugged. "This system is great for cutthroats. We've never tried it with grayling. That's the kind of thing we really need you in here for. Just to see what happens."

The biosaddles in the other buckets looked black and empty, no silt to speak of. The thermometer read fortythree degrees. I opened up my logbook and on the waxy, waterproof paper jotted the date and time, and then my day's work. "Water 43, steady rain, stream flow same, little to no sediment." Like my last egg job, it didn't seem the workload would bury me.

Back at the horses, we shook hands, and Lee climbed onto Gus. "Only twenty more miles," I said.

Lee rolled his eyes and Tom muttered about foot soldiers. He shook my hand, saddling up while holding the pack string's lead rope. He'd be back in a month to pick me up. If the grayling hatched by then. "Enjoy yourself back here," he said. "Any last questions?"

"How's your head?"

"Could've been worse," he said, then glanced around, into the dark trees. "How much do you actually know about bears?"

"Save the last shot for yourself?"

He smiled. "I don't usually get too nervous, but this is not good country to be alone in. Especially this time of year."

It seemed an odd time to bring this up.

"Climb a tree if you get the chance. Your pepper spray." He glanced into the gloomy drip of trees hemming the trail. "Best thing is to avoid them altogether. Make a lot of noise. Wherever you can't see. Like here, going in to the eggs."

Before, by the creek, I hadn't been able to hear Tom shouting. Maybe bears had better ears. I wasn't even sure *how* to make a lot of noise. My whole life in the woods had been built around quiet, stealth even, seeing what I could see. Climb a tree? I pictured trying to shimmy up the skinny, blackened, branchless trunks in the burn. Only an islander, a lifetime of coconuts behind him, would have a chance. "Okay," I said.

"Use the radio in the cabin if you need anything," Tom said. "Don't be shy about that." He'd gone over radio procedures after breakfast. "And check in. Every day. Let us know you're okay."

He gave a last look around and said, "Well, you take care of yourself."

"And my eggs," Lee added.

I stood off the trail, hip boots squelching. The pack loads clinked and creaked as they started away, the smell of wet horses not all that different from wet dog. I fell in step behind them, walking a hundred yards downstream to Tom's crossing tree, a barkless snag spanning the creek, a double-trunker. The crossing, even on muddy, felt-bottomed boots, the creek racing by three feet below, was hardly a tightrope stunt.

13

Bob Marshall Wilderness, Montana
May 2004

Safe on my side of the creek, I turn to watch the last of the pack string slog up out of the creek bottom and climb up the Ireland green of the hill until they crest and disappear. I stand a moment more, looking at the empty hillside in the drizzle, the deep brown line of empty trail snaking up it. Then I turn and start up the rocky patch of creek bank to my boots, the long walk back.

Sitting on a log beside my boots, I shuck off my hip boots and squish back into my sodden Gore-Tex, glance back over my shoulder at the empty trail. I push myself up, icy water squelching between my toes. The rain hums down. Fog hangs in what timber I can see. Gray on gray on gray.

I start walking, the only person out here. One foot forward into the mud, then the other.

The trail climbs, flecked with river stone, plowed into long muddy slides by the horses. One step forward, two steps back, I pick my way from rock to rock, grabbing tree branches, rosebushes, downed logs. I slip to a knee, clutch a brittle knot of snowberry, dig my cold toes into the mud, and hang on, each breath adding its own cloud of fog to the air.

Eventually I fight my way out of the creek cut, and the wind pelts straight into my face, shoving me back. I see the wall of rain ahead, watch it race toward me, the grass of Biggs Flat whipping before it like a living, writhing thing. I pull up my hood, and it hits, slapping my coat against me, flapping it like wings. I lower my head, brace myself, bare hand up on a burned tree trunk, the wet charcoal glistening, and then set off, every step taking me deeper into the wilderness.

In the lull between gusts, I glance around, though I can't see much beyond a hundred yards, the blur of rain, the closed world inside the clouds. For all I can tell I might as well have never left Wisconsin, might still be twelve years old, trudging across Wisconsin prairie, and then, suddenly, I am.

There's an air base there, or half of one, Bong, named not for the pot-smoking device I'd be confronted with soon enough, but for the top U.S. ace of World War II, killed test-flying a jet fighter on the day the *Enola Gay* dropped its load on Hiroshima. A decade later, the military began building the base for jet fighters, then decided it wasn't needed. Construction ceased, leaving a vast expanse of open federal ground, a couple of rusty, bullet-holed fuel tanks, some half-dozed gravelly airstrips, lots of ponds. Taken over by a few lonely model-rocket enthusiasts, radio-control airplane fliers, it was a place we could launch my brother's three-foot-tall, two-stage, blue-and-white barber-poled rocket and chase after it without fear of crossing roads or fences in the miles it took to drift back to earth.

We fired smaller rockets, bounding after them like deer, but it was Paul's I remembered best, stretching the ignition wires as far as they would reach, a little trepidation seeping in as we fitted the size D rocket into its firing nozzle, the smaller second-stage rocket into its place.

Some of the rocket details escaped over the years, but what never left was what followed that swooshing rush of a successful ignition, the paper tube zooming off, no tonnage to reenact the *Saturn V*'s slow-building lift. My father and brothers and I, necks cricked back, squinted into the blue, the rocket already hard to see, when suddenly a puff of white smoke signaled a proper separation, the firing of the second engine. A moment or two later, the quick whisk of sound reached down to us, the thin, rapier-like second-stage knifing completely out of sight, the four of us staring into empty sky, waiting for the engine to burn out, for the red-and-white chute to pop open, something big enough for us to see, my dad trying to keep an eye on the tumbling first stage, responsibility incarnate.

And then the best part: spying the chute, waiting to judge the direction of wind drift, my father pointing, showing which way to head, cutting us loose like hounds on a blood scent. We tore headlong through the scrub and weed, running, falling, laughing, scrambling back up, our faces turned to the sky, not to our footing or path. A lone barbed wire fence would have beheaded the three of us. My father followed more slowly, trying to keep us in sight, the rocket too. Our dog bounded along with us, unable to believe that we'd been allowed, however briefly, to join her species.

We splashed through the soggy low spots with glee, but the first time we reached a real body of water, reedy edges, open blue in the middle, we paused, judging the necessary detour, looking back at our dad, wondering. I could still feel the drop of my jaw when he shrugged and, after the briefest hesitation, waved us forward, right through the center of the pond.

Already gasping from the run, we splashed into ankle-deep water, knee-deep, howling with laughter. Then thigh-deep, and, biting our lips, straining on tiptoe, crotch, waist, belly, our dash slowed to a slog. I can't remember now if a crawdad actually found its way into one of our pants, or if it was only a joke, something we suffered to breathe through, giggling ourselves sick over what it might latch its claws onto.

"Swamp crawling" we dubbed this new, undreamed-of sport, and, for me at least, the firing of the rocket became only an excuse for that heedless charge, the rescinding of all rules of normal comportment, of all rules of any kind. A pond? Run through it. Jeans? Sweatshirts? Boots? No matter. Swim if you have to. You know how. Climb dripping out the other side, stagger on, water draining down your pants legs, squelching out of your ruined boots. Who cares? Try not to howl, not to let loose the wildness you feel building inside you, a rush unknown, unsuspected, something you've yet to understand, at twelve years old, that you will crave for the rest of your days. Then realize you have no

reason to hold it in: there are no rules here, no compunc-
tions. So you howl, scream like a madman, glance over at
your brothers and realize that they're staring at you, laughing
like demons, that they can't believe you're screaming, and
then they are, too. You can hardly run, hardly stand, hardly
breathe for sheer exhilaration. You look back to your
father—the enforcer of Saturday-morning jobs, a man who
could stand in front of a cartoon-filled TV screen holding
up a Popsicle stick, informing you that he'd found it next to
the waste basket, *on the floor,* make you get up and put it in
correctly—and he is at least as delighted, seeing you, his son,
gone feral before his very eyes. You cannot believe your
luck, your amazing good fortune. You grin back, the briefest flash of teeth, of open mouth, then charge forward again.
There's a rocket out there somewhere, or, if not really a
rocket, something. Something you will be chasing for the
rest of your life.

Thirty-three years later, I trudge alone through the rain,
squelching water inside my worthless boots, pushing elk out
ahead of me, the new snow on the mountains deepening but
hidden, as are any nearby grizzlies, by the fog and clouds.
The last time we ever saw Paul's rocket was high above
Bong, our wild charge slowed by the fact that we'd reached
a point directly beneath the rocket, that it was no longer
drifting in any direction. Our dad caught up with us, the
four of us straining to see the red-and-white parachute, its
cargo already too far away to pick out. It was my father
who first noticed that instead of enlarging, the chute was
actually shrinking. "It's going up," he said. The parachute,
still tantalizingly straight above us, grew tinier and tinier as

our father, the engineer, talked about thermals, rising masses of hot air, the give-and-take of heat exchange.

Then it was gone. We scanned the empty blue, swirls and blots dancing, our eyes making dots where none existed, but the parachute, Paul's rocket, never reappeared. I should have known then. But, as quick on the uptake as ever, it is only half a life later, a mile from Biggs Creek in the Bob Marshall Wilderness, that I pinpoint that vanishing rocket as the start of that life, the moment that led to Montana, to Indian Creek, to here.

Slipping and stumbling in the mud and grass, I wonder what my dad would have to say to that shrug of his, that nod into a pond, leading me so far off the beaten paths—if, given a glimpse into the future, he'd do it again.

The glimpse is impossible of course. Who could tell, looking at a breathless, tousle-haired kid staring up into the sky, water draining out of his burr-speckled jeans, that a world had just opened to him, when the kid himself would take thirty-some years to realize it? But, it's still what I want to do for my boys at every sliver of opportunity. Let them take the oars, then jump overboard. "Here's the knife. Try not to cut yourself." Toss them the ball and tell them, "Throw me some smoke. Make my hand burn. Don't, ever, worry about me."

I slog on without them, not twelve, not in Wisconsin, just forty-five and wet and tired and alone in the wilderness. *This is who you are.* But, without them, is it who I want to be?

14

Bob Marshall Wilderness, Montana
May 2004

As I march, I work on math. One month out here. A seventieth of Aidan's life, a hundredth of Nolan's. A mere five hundredth of mine. Maybe this is all something I should have calculated before.

Indian Creek, sure, I'd been twenty, footloose, clueless, reading far too many mountain man books. What was seven months then? But now? Miss the last of Aidan's kindergarten? Both their baseball seasons? I'm the coach, for crying out loud.

I've been hiking five hours by the time I slip and slide down to the pack bridge, then claw and pull my way back up the ridge above the river for Spruce Creek. I'm pushing on my thighs, plodding, looking nowhere but at the ground, my next step. Heavy with water, my hood hangs as low before my eyes as a sullen teenager's hair. The drum of rain against it lulls me into something near a trance. One foot forward, then the other. I slog through the thick trees hardly noticing their dark menace in the overall gloom, not making a sound, not a glance left or right.

At Spruce I make the descent on my ass, a semicontrolled pinball off the clot of charcoaled snags. The eggs are the same: pink, eyed, tiny. I have to look a long time to see one vibrate. No silt to swirl, I look back up the hill, pull myself to my feet on another tilted, blackened snag, and start the struggle up the mud-wracked, burned, and broken slope.

Reaching the top, I hunch over, hands on knees, sucking air like a wounded marathoner. Soaked with rain and sweat, globbed with mud, and smudged black from the sodden charcoal of the snags, every line and crease of my hands etched sooty from grabbing and pulling myself up and over them, I hang my head, feel the charge of my pulse. I've walked maybe ten miles. Ten. I'd left the boys to wear myself out in nothing more than ten miles? In the twenty-five years since Indian Creek, have I grown nothing but old?

I straighten, push my hood back enough so I can see, no trace of sun, the clouds only feet above me, thick and heavy as wool, and there in the trail, I stare down at a grizzly track, stark in the mud, covering my own boot print, a whole series of them, a quiet amble up the river, right behind me, middle of the day.

I turn, look behind me, out into the rain, my gut tightening. I'd been down at the river what, ten minutes? fifteen?

I think of my mindless plod through the thick stretch and wonder just how much older I'm going to get.

But can I really walk miles a day the way Lee had, shouting, "Hey, bear! Hey, Boo-Boo?" at every dark spot in the trail? For the next month? Clapping four or five hours a day? Whistling a happy tune?

Instead, wavery at first, but louder and stronger as the trail gets tighter and even gloomier, my view shorter, I sing. More limited than my talent, though, is my repertoire, every song I'd ever heard driven out of my head by the repetition of the few bedtime songs I'd croaked out for the last eight years. Entering the blackest stretches of timber, I belt out: "Fox Went Out on a Chilly Night," or "The Noble Duke of York," or "The Bear Went Over the Mountain," a natural, "Momma's Little Baby Loves Shortnin' Bread," "Take Me Out to the Ball Game." But, still, they're our bedtime songs. I can hardly make it through them.

Safely back into the burn where I can see, I shut up, sliding down the greasy trail to the pack bridge. I pause halfway across, leaning over the rail, watching the swollen river tear along, a filthy runoff brown, fishing a long way off. I trudge on, my boots ringing hollowly on the planking until I hit the mud on the other side and start the climb.

I puff up the hill above the river, then drop into the last deep, dark, dripping forest, the Gates Creek waterfall loud enough to muffle whatever the rain doesn't. The bears' favorite trail to the river.

I try singing the boys their songs, but my voice gives up completely and I plug along, wiping the rain from my face with my sooty hands. A month out here without them? I can't strangle out one more word. Let the bears eat me.

Longest last few miles in my history.

Then, at last, there sit the squat, dark buildings, the tangle of willows and beaver ponds, a whitetail bounding away from the tree edges, a few elk glancing up from the airstrip.

I push the last hundred yards, unshutter the east window, clomp up onto the porch for that window. A robin blows out of a nest in the eaves, startling me as witless as I've spooked her. I shuffle across the boards, open that shutter, unlock the door. But I don't go in. I know the gloom of the empty, cold, half-shuttered cabin will be deadly. Instead, I continue around, opening the west window, the west door, before walking inside. No hubbub now, no trail-boss breakfast bowing the table legs. Just nothing.

I sit on the table bench, my feet pruned inside my boots. I undo the Velcro seams of my rain pants. Unlace my boots. More mud. I hang my raincoat up on a nail, listen to it drip with the steadiness of a nighttime faucet. I kick my boots off beside the stove, soggy footprints marking my path as I rebuild the fire and cross to the bed and collapse.

The short night, the warden's eating-as-endurance event, the newness, the rain, the long, soggy slog, and, most of all, the smack in the face of solitude gang up on me, wearing me down as surely as a stick against a sidewalk. I knew I'd face this, was even expecting it, just not quite this hard emptiness of it all. I didn't expect, with a single glance at an old Batman pillow, to find myself barely able to swallow, let alone breathe.

But, after lying there a minute, the threat of the emptiness swallowing me whole, I push myself up to my elbows, look around the empty cabin, and say, out loud, "It's okay. You've been here before."

And I have. So many times. My last fall in college, I managed a schedule that left me with classes only on Tuesdays and Thursdays. So every Thursday afternoon I left Missoula to roam a huge expanse of open ground across the divide, camping beside a creek thick with beaver and muskrat, roaming the mountains day after day with vague hopes of bouncing up flocks of sharptails or Hungarian partridge, maybe some blues or ruffed grouse. More often than not, come Monday, I could find no reason to go back to Missoula for just one day of class, and, well, Wednesday held the same problem. I often skipped the whole week, stayed out ten days or more, eating oatmeal and rice, birds, fish, the occasional muskrat. Once, in an early, driving snow, I heard what I took to be gunshots, but in all my time in this place I had never seen another person before the big game season, and curiosity drove me across mountains and creek cuts to find not hunters but massive-horned rams rearing back and charging across low, snow-clumped bunchgrass, banging their heads into each other, standing back quivering, shocked, then backing up and doing it again, the stunning bone-on-bone collisions echoing up the canyons into the low, gray sky, into me.

But every first night out there, a sleeping bag in the grass, a tiny twig fire to poke at, the mournful honking of migrating snow geese drifting down from the stars, these attacks of loneliness, or some cousin of it, would close around me like the darkness, leaving me wondering what I might be missing back with my friends, wondering what it was that drew me so determinedly out here, away from everything. It was a need I pinned vaguely to my months at Indian Creek, some virus of isolation I'd been infected with there, something malarial, flaring up now and then, leaving me fevered for solitude, then subsiding into its dormant phase of near normalcy.

After school, my seasonal river-ranger job in the Tetons left a gap of five unemployed months every winter. By February, I'd be hiking up the Van Buren entrance ramp in Missoula, mittened thumb out, sign strapped to my backpack, big black Sharpie letters. LARAMIE, for a game warden exam. DENVER, for a girlfriend in the ski hills west of town. UTAH, when Rader was working in Bryce Canyon. VEGAS, to see my old boss at Lake Mead. TEXAS, for my sister outside Galveston. The destination was never as important as the leaving, the moving. Mardi Gras was supposed to be worth the trip, wasn't it? LOUISIANA. I slept at friends' when it worked or in the roadside snow or sage. Once, dropped off after midnight by a driver who'd realized he'd taken a wrong turn, I stumbled through the snow and the dark to get away from the highway and threw down my sleeping bag outside what was, I wouldn't discover until dawn's light, the edge of a horserace track outside Buffalo, Wyoming. The stars burned pinpricks through the night, and I have never been so cold, pulling every bit of clothing out of my pack, putting my down jacket over my bag, waiting for the first traces of light, when I could see what I was getting into. Stashed in the foot of my sleeping bag, my water bottle froze solid anyway, and at dawn I staggered into town, into the first café I found, spooking the waitress, who begged me to tell her

I had not been outside last night, who filled and refilled my coffee cup as fast as she could, threw bacon and eggs and hash browns at me, would not take a dime.

Even so, there was never an exit harder to reach than that first one in Missoula, already missing all I was leaving, already wondering what was wrong with me, what drove me so. But, too long in any one place, I began to itch. The reason never stated, never thought out, I just had to move. There was more out there, so much more, things I'd never seen or heard or felt, even dreamed of. How, with all of that, could anyone sit still?

And yet at the start of every trip, every first night alone, lay that, that what? Not loneliness exactly, but a blend of uncertainty, and wondering, and missing already what I'd only just left behind, which was maybe the same thing. I'd learned over the years that the treatment, if not the cure, was action. Keep yourself busy, don't go idle, do not let the tendrils of loneliness take root, the creepers of doubt begin to weave their stranglehold. At Indian Creek it was firewood cutting that got me through the first, hardest days, cord after cord, old snags felled, limbed, bucked, carried one chunk at a time to the truck, driven back to my tent one truckload after another. Unloaded, split, stacked, one row of log halves, another of quarters, another of kindling. Forty cubic meters of wood.

Staring up at the whitewashed ceiling planks of the Gates Park cabin, I force myself to my feet. A floorboard creaks, oak, its finish long, long gone, the place emptily, eerily quiet. I take a deep breath, a look around. Firewood already in abundance, there's only food to be cached, tools to unload, clothes to unpack. All just stuff for myself, not the three of us.

I can hardly imagine starting.

I edge one foot forward, the other, walk outside, cross to the bunkhouse, jab the key at the lock, prop open the door with an ax to let in a little light. My second dry bag hangs back in the shadows. Waiting for the okay for the boys, I'd left spots open for their stuff until the very end and now have no clear idea of what finally went where.

I throw the sixty-pound pack onto my shoulders and totter out, away from the gloom.

In the light of the main cabin, I drop the pack beside its twin and force myself to sit long enough to eat, though I can't quite keep from hunching over the pack while choking down the last bites, fumbling one-handed with the straps, rolling open the waterproof flaps.

The food inside is bundled in black garbage bags, as if I'd been setting out on a river expedition. A force of habit. I set them aside. Hauling out my clothes, I glance around for some sort of closet. A splintery plywood box mounted on casters sits squeezed beneath my bunk, as close to mouse-proof as I'll get. I roll it out, find only a Pulaski and a couple of split fire-hose crosscut saw guards. I sort my clothes by weather group: shorts and T-shirts, which now seem more than optimistic, then jeans and wool shirts, jackets and caps, socks and gloves.

Diving into the second pack, after the routine of straps and flaps, something I've closed and opened thousands of times, the first thing I uncover is a tin of Jiffy Pop. Then another.

Popcorn. Aidan's favorite food. They hadn't been there when I rolled the flap shut, cinched down the straps.

I lift out each tin and find a paper napkin stained green and black with felt tips, a picture of me riding away atop a loaded packhorse, entering a narrow lane between thick stands of dark green pines. Oddly like the top of the hill above the lake. A shaky arrow points to a tiny figure curled up in the horse's pack. "ME," it says. Nolan's dream of stowing away.

I try for a breath, whatever advantage I'd gained by staying busy whisked straight away. I glance around the empty cabin, crowded with nothing but my scattered, ragged gear, and sink down onto the table's long bench. The Jiffy Pop dangles from my fingers.

Ever since they started school I've drawn cartoons like this on their lunch napkins, something from their day of school when I can: a test paper covered with red marks, a violin playing itself on the night of a concert, or, if they've got a game or meet, a bare-bunned kid holding up his suit, a flaming baseball screaming off their Little League bat, or, if nothing comes to mind, superheroes or Orcs, upcoming holidays, a turkey hiding behind the chopping block, Santa with a broken sleigh, made-up monsters, anything. Every day.

I hear Rose saying I had to have a life apart from them, words that missed anything left inside me by light-years. Who I was should have been the person helping him into that horse pack, helping him stow away, doing whatever it took to make his dreams come true. And here I sit with his good-bye note, only the dripping of my rain gear surrounding me.

I set the napkin and popcorn on the table, force myself through a couple of pacing laps around the cabin. In, then out. Breathing can't be that hard. Another lap. I pick up the popcorn and slip it into a drawer, store the napkin in my wallet, where I have never carried any photos. Batman watches my every move from his place on my bunk. I tuck my sleeping bag over him.

"Okay," I say out loud. "Okay." I grab a garbage bag full of food and get out, carry it down toward the creek, the food cache. Scraping away a spot in the mouse turds, I stake my claim, building a tower based on the impenetrable cans of corn and peas, setting my apples and carrots on top, guessing it would be small deterrence to the mice.

Stepping out, sucking in the fresh air, I drag my pack of dried food to the bunkhouse, lob it up onto the hanging platform along with a year or two's worth of other such supplies.

In the cabin, it only takes a few minutes to get my books stashed, my journal pads and pens set up in the corner of the desk beneath the radio, just past the head of my bed.

Then I'm finished. Moved in. Nothing left to do.

I glance around the still, quiet cabin, spot the mop and broom by the back door, and leap for them as if for a life ring, whip the broom across the floor, gather the collection of mud we'd left the night before. I push open the back door to sweep the porch, the robin and I scaring the hell out of each other again. I wonder how long it's been since anybody swept this porch, glad no one would catch me at it.

I fill a pot for mopping, set it sizzling on the stove. Waiting, I wipe the table, stack the spices and condiments, steak sauces and Tabasco onto the little lazy Susan, pushing it back beneath the window, beside the decks of worn cards, the stack of cribbage boards.

I dip my finger in the pot on the stove. Close enough. I start slopping the big string mop back and forth, the tang of damp oak rising.

The weather turns windy, the overcast almost blown open in gaps, though still no trace of sun makes it through. But, with both doors open, the floor dries nearly as soon as I swipe the mop over it. Letting it air, I head to the woodpile on the far side of the bunkhouse and, needed or not, set to splitting a new load of kindling for the stove. I lug over a full stack of big logs too, until the wood box can take no more. Except for my filthy, soggy socks hanging from the drying wire, the place is spotless.

I stand then in the doorway, studying the bunkhouse, the outhouse, the corrals, the airstrip. The wind, still heavy with wet, sends a shiver through me. I close the door, stoke the fire, which no matter how I draw it out, only takes a minute.

Shaking my head, I push the stove door shut, lock down the handle. I'm acting like I've been hermitted up for years, not, I glance at my watch, six hours.

I pull a wool shirt out of my closet, then another, slip them on, button them up. Taking my fly rod off the nails above the window, where it's rested for maybe an hour,

I start out, past the short, single-rail fence surrounding the cabin, and down past the food cache to the creek, what seemed to be mostly a mass of swampy willow and flooded beaver ponds, but here a manageable six-foot-wide stream, riffling through a couple of curves, pooling up in others. In the Tetons, the river had been full of Snake River cutthroat, suckers for a yellow humpy. I tie one on and work out a little line.

Just the act of casting, the rhythmic give-and-take, no matter how worn out I am, lets me catch my breath, ease back my shoulders.

Standing back on the pebbles, making the distance almost twelve feet, I drop the fly against the undercut bank across from me. It drifts an inch, maybe two, and disappears in a swirl. I set the hook, the little flick of rod tip enough to send four inches of cutthroat skittering across the surface to the rocks at my feet. Dropping the rod tip, giving him slack, he shakes and is off, darting across to his spot beneath the bank.

I sit, and the sun pokes through for a moment, letting me see ten or so trout lined out just above the narrowing, fast water leading to the next pool. More four-to-six-inchers, but a couple of meat eaters going seven, maybe eight.

I put the fly in front of them, let it drift, watch them dart at it, one after another, some taking a stab, some coming in for a closer look but rejecting at the last second. I move to the water's edge again and again, wetting my hand, slipping out the hook, letting the fish slide back into their slots in the current.

After introducing myself to every fish there, I start

upstream, making casts now and then, missing, against a small dead pine down in the water, what feels like the biggest fish yet. But the missed one's always the biggest. Long stretches of apparently perfect water seem to hold no fish at all; then suddenly there's a bend or drop teeming with the little trout.

Crossing and recrossing the creek, I push my way through the willow tangles and find myself at the base of an enormous beaver dam, the creek trickling through its woven-together sticks and logs, gathering into the channel I'd followed up. Grass and moss and young willows grow up from the face of the dam, something that's been here for years, decades, and I look up at its top, higher than my head, more little runs of water flowing over here and there. Though I'm too low to see the surface of the pond, there's a huge absence there, no willow tops, no trees reaching into the sky, only a lone pine snag, gray and dead and drowned, and I guess the pond must be the Lake Mead of beaver ponds, a huge expanse of water, loaded with who knows what. Cutthroat, beaver, ducks. Muskrat maybe. Otter.

But, instead of climbing up the dam or trekking around it to the high ground, the run of lodgepole curbing the south side, I hesitate, simply stand before it. I don't know if it's obsession or habit or simply a superstition, my own rabbit's foot to rub or something that actually makes sense, but in my time in the wilds I've learned to always hold something in reserve, something for when things might get harder. So snowshoeing along the Selway at twenty below, I'd leave my jacket a bit unzipped, or carry my hat in my pocket, something saved for when it got colder, for when the wind picked up. Or rounding a mountain lake, stooping down to search for skipping stones, I'd find the perfect skipper, an aerodynamic marvel, and instead of launching it, I'd pocket it, skip all its inferior rivals instead, saving the perfect stone for the perfect time, the perfect place. Maybe it made no sense at all; maybe it was all a holdout from childhood, stretching and stretching the Halloween candy until, in December, I'd have to hold the last stale Tootsie Rolls in my mouth a while just to soften them enough to bite into. Now here, my first day in, I don't want to discover everything yet. I want, as always, more, and more, and I pocket the chance to explore the mother of all beaver ponds for a later, maybe harder day. Just something in reserve, to hold on to, to anticipate and savor.

So I turn away, retrace my steps down the little channel toward the food cache, then bushwhack through the willows, popping out on the sagebrush bench just behind the corrals, and, guessing I might be high enough to see the pond, I keep my back turned, don't even chance a peek back that way. Instead, the sun breaks through, widening stretches of blue between the clouds, clouds that are more white than gray, and I take that, a pretty evening to walk through, until, slowly, I reach the empty cabin.

After picking through some Fish and Game leftovers, I find myself just sitting at the long table, chin propped on a fist, looking out the window, the first few elk coming out into the grass on the airstrip. I lose track of the time, barely notice the gloom of dusk settle around me.

I pull the Batman pillow out, straighten my bed. I think of Tom and Lee shuffling around here, readying for bed, only last night. My first nights at Indian Creek, still surrounded by the wardens and hunters, I'd been awed by how much they knew, how much they seemed to fit there, as much a part of the mountains as the trees and the rock. Only decades later did I learn that they'd been equally awed, knowing that they were leaving in days, that I was staying in.

But, really, it's the boys I think about, their room, the small single beds, one on each wall, the empty rocking chair in between, my spot. I turn the lever on the lantern, let the darkness sweep in. Let its hiss ebb away.

15

The road toward the boys started, I suppose, the spring before Indian Creek, with Rader bursting into our dorm room at a little after ten on a Saturday night. I'd just dragged myself back from a ten-hour shift of lifeguarding at the Grizzly Pool, had just managed to untie my shoes. He'd been at a dorm function all night, a barbecue and keg up at Fort Fizzle, the little picnic ground up on Lolo Creek, where a militia had utterly failed to stop Chief Joseph and his Nez Perce a hundred years earlier. Rader had become enamored, and now everyone was heading out dancing. The object of his sudden affection waited down in the parking lot, in his station wagon, the Deerslayer. So did her inseparable companion.

"Great," I said. "Have fun."

"You've got to come."

"I'm done. Wiped."

"You have to come. You have to pry off this other girl."

I shook my head. "Exhausted. Finished." I lay back on the bed, felt myself sink in.

He made promises, wilder and wilder, started putting my shoes back on my feet. I sighed, sat up. "Okay, okay," I said, pushing him away, tying my shoes myself. I dragged downstairs after him, off to meet these beauties.

The bar was hopping, people jitterbugging across the floor, the band deafening. Rader led us to the Fort Fizzle table, pitchers of beer, plastic glasses. We found chairs. Rader jumped up with his crush to hit the dance floor. Her inseparable partner asked me, and I shook my head. More and more emphatically. The girl across the table smiled. "Don't dance, huh?"

"Nope."

"Want a beer?"

I rubbed at my face. "Not really." But that smile.

She smiled wider. "Well, how about a shot then?"

By the end, Rader pulling me away, out of the chair I hadn't left all night, I leaned across the table, shouting over the band, "What's your name?"

She shouted something back. I shook my head. "Your name! I need to know your name!"

She laughed, leaned closer, within reach. "Rose," she yelled.

A brighter bulb might have thought to ask for a phone number. I didn't see her again until the next fall, just after I'd accepted the Indian Creek job. Just a glimpse, passing near the food service, but when I shouted her name, she turned, the same smile, the same shake of her head. "Pete," she said. We had one date before I left for the wilderness. For seven months.

Which became something of a pattern for us.

I came back to school. She took the quarter off.

I went to New Zealand. She went to Ireland.

I returned to Missoula for my last year. She'd transferred to Bozeman.

I called her home in Butte, got her Bozeman address, stopped by on my way off to somewhere. Nobody home. I crawled through a window. I got in a car wreck hitchhiking to Wyoming. Bleary and concussed, I roamed across Bozeman in a blizzard, jimmied the door lock, was asleep on the couch when she and her roommates stumbled in after midnight. They flipped on the light, spotted me on the couch. Her roommate said, "Rosie, that guy's here again."

I heard a lot about bad timing, about what a good guy I was, but . . . Again and again over the years. I thought a lot about African wild dogs, their relentless patience, the inexorable pursuit.

And then, five years into the African-wild-dog courtship, she flinched. Invited by a friend to a party in Missoula, she asked if I was still working in the Tetons. She wondered if I'd mind if she took a summer job there, working for the lodge company.

If I'd *mind*?

That whole summer, when she threw off her apron and wiped the lettuce from her hands, ready to dash away at the end of every shift, if anyone asked what she was doing, she'd shout back over her shoulder, "The ranger!"

We floated the Snake in every spare moment. Or broke

out, off to the Buffalo Fork, the Green, or up into Montana, the Big Hole, the Yellowstone, the Missouri. Or we'd leave behind the boats and the park, all its rules, and tear off for more wide-open wilderness, backpack in as far as we could, eat brook trout, throw our bags out by the fire—a tent, even a flashlight, beyond my financial reach. We hiked up to catch the ice out at Jade Lake, not quite timing it just right, post-holing through knee-deep snow the last mile. Rose's tennis shoes became packed with the icy crystals of corn snow. She pointed out that my knee-high boots hadn't.

The Wind River Range became our favorite, a willingness to drop or climb away from the popular trails leading to complete solitude. A map would have helped, would have foretold the two-thousand-foot drops, the three-thousand-foot climbs. Cramming hikes into short days off, we left at shift's end, hiked the first set of switchbacks, which were down, not up. We camped beside a creek, the cold settling heavy into the bottom. Up at dawn, coffee over a twig fire, we tackled the next set of switchbacks, which were up, and up, and up. Maybe five miles down the first evening, five more up, another few up top, till we found the little lake, teeming with brook trout. We cooked them over more twigs, stayed too long, started back, the whole way, a twenty-mile round-trip. Down and down and down, back to the creek, and then back up, already fifteen miles under our belts. It started to rain. The mosquitoes homed in. We plodded on, conversation at a minimum. Every time I looked back, swatting more mosquitoes off my knuckles, Rose smiled up, sweat and rain streaking her face, ratting her hair.

"Okay?"

"Great."

The last few miles blurred, as much by exhaustion as rain. Thumbs hooked under shoulder straps, we trudged, stopped at trickling little streams for drinks, pushed back up, back on. Then, finally, the flat, packed dirt supertrail leading to the parking lot, to civilization. I dropped the tailgate of my truck, and we shrugged out of our packs. I retrieved the cooler from the front, cracked a no-longer-cold one, and passed it to Rose for the first sip. I held it, waiting, as she concentrated on easing off her boot, the same kind of Red Wing work boot I wore. Her gray wool sock was red. Not just tinged, blushed, but red, crimson. I helped her peel off the sock, revealing the burst remains of huge blisters on her heels, the balls of her feet. They looked skinned. "Jesus," I said, "why didn't you say something?"

"What would we have done? Stopped?" She shrugged, took the beer, sipped, let out a long "Aaaaaah!"

She limped around to the cab of the truck. "We should probably go find something colder."

The year she graduated from school, engineering degree in hand, Rose and I took a two-month-long winter road trip, another of my disintegrating trucks, a Ford Courier this time. The Tour de National Park she called it. Yellowstone, Tetons, Rocky Mountain, Bryce, Zion, Mesa Verde, Aransas Wildlife Refuge to see the whoopers, Padre Island National Seashore. All wending our way down toward New Orleans, Mardi Gras, interstates only when no other roads existed. We wore out our atlas, took stabs in the

dark, little more than educated guesses. All roads had to go
somewhere, no?

Rounding around the Gulf toward New Orleans, trying
to stay on the water's edge, we finally came up against one
that didn't go anywhere. A giant sign, billboard-size, stood
planted into the actual asphalt itself. ROAD CLOSED NEXT 25
MILES. HURRICANE DAMAGE.

We stopped, idling in front of it. We checked the map,
measured the backtracking, the circling around, murmuring
curses. I got out, walked to the sign, peered around it down
the long, empty road. It looked pretty solid to me.

I came back, said so. Rose raised an eyebrow.

"Well, we could just go down a ways. See."

"And just have to backtrack that much more?"

I shrugged. "Maybe."

"Look at that sign. It's permanent. You think the road's
fine?"

I shrugged again. "We could find out."

She shook her head, told me I was an idiot, some such
sweet nothing.

I edged to the shoulder, off it, praying we wouldn't get
stuck in the sand. Then around the sign, back up onto the
pavement, the empty road stretched out before us, our own
private coastal yellow brick road, gilded with sand edging
across it here and there, but gradually our speed crept up.
Windows rolled down, the salt air against our skins, we
flew, driving in either lane, down the center, the only people
on the planet. Two miles, five miles. I laughed and laughed,
and Rose smiled, wondering what the same road would

look like coming back, after we reached, at last, the washed-out section.

Ten miles. Arms resting out the windows, the wind and sun streaming through, our hair flying, the ocean's slow rolls glinting, almost within reach. Twelve miles. Twelve and a half. "Halfway!" I crowed.

At about thirteen the engine coughed. A little jerk up against the seat belts. A glance at each other. It did it again, bucking and sputtering. And then, poof, nothing. The sound suddenly only the wind, dying out as we coasted, and then, as we rolled to a stop, only the slow, easy lap of the surf.

Before she could say a word, I said, "We are not out of gas."

"Great," she said.

I looked ahead, avoiding the stare. Tried the key. It ground and ground, but nothing kicked, no fire to the engine. That pretty much exhausted my mechanical expertise. Beside me, Rose said, "You have got to be shitting me."

I got out. Lifted the hood. Wiggled some wires. Pulled on a belt or two. All shipshape. "Try it again," I called.

The little breeze off the Gulf didn't give much relief from the heat, the humidity.

The engine cranked and cranked. Nothing.

"It's like it's not getting any gas," I said.

With the hood up, I couldn't see Rose. This was not a terrible thing.

I took the lid off the carburetor. Stared at it. Following hoses down and back, I found what I guessed might be the fuel pump, oddly enough, bolted onto the frame under the driver's seat. More tubing ran from it toward the gas tank. I was onto something. "Maybe it's the fuel pump. Maybe just a clogged filter."

"What do you know about fuel pumps?" Rose asked. She sat in the cab, making tuna fish sandwiches, her lap her plate and cutting board. At least we wouldn't starve. Not yet.

Working with my Swiss Army knife, the lone crescent wrench I'd found in the glove box, I managed to get the hose leading to the engine off, found a filter, which, unfortunately, looked fairly pristine. I asked Rose to crank it again, and she did, with only a minor eye roll. Nothing came out of the pump. "Pump's not working," I said.

"Got an extra?"

That was pretty hysterical. I pulled the hose off the gas-tank side of the pump. Maybe the obstruction was between the tank and the pump and the pump really was just fine. I closed my lips over the tubing, gave a little suck. Nothing. I sucked harder. Still nothing. The problem all but diagnosed, I gave a mighty pull and more gasoline than I ever wanted in my mouth gushed straight in.

I staggered back, spitting and gagging, pulling up my shirt to wipe my tongue on it. Eyes watering too hard to see, I cried for water.

Rose grabbed the first thing she could and, tuna fish still on her lap, she passed me the carton of orange juice that had been lying on the floorboards all day, the one we suspected had gone bad, now heated to ninety-some degrees. I gulped in a load as mouthwash, expecting water, and it launched out as violently as the gasoline, some out my nose.

I crawled in circles on my hands and knees, the asphalt burning in the sun, mouth open, spitting, drooling, stomach turning.

When at last I caught my breath, managed not to puke, I sat back and said, "What on earth did you give me?"

She told me, and I blinked, rubbed the tears from my eyes. "Orange juice?" I said.

"Kind of like a screwdriver, you know?"

I sat on the asphalt, my rear heating, and nodded.

"How's that pump?"

"I think I got it," I said.

Avoiding the bright-orange puddles on the road, I went back to work, reconnecting everything I'd taken apart. I lifted the water jug out of the back of the truck, rinsed and rinsed and rinsed. Everything I would ever eat, from now until the end of time, would taste like a refinery.

Instead of having Rose crank a dead engine again, I said I'd do it. She shoved over, held a sandwich out to me like a question. The reek of canned tuna did nothing to enhance the taste of gasoline. The atlas sat between us, rolled tight. In case the truck didn't start, I supposed.

I turned the key and the engine fired, first try. Well, second maybe.

I pushed it into gear, smiled, baring my fumy teeth, and pushed down the gas. We were off.

"We're going forward?"

"Brilliant," I said.

"But . . ."

"We're more than halfway."

She lowered the sandwich. "Really?"

"We'll be fine," I said.

And we were, the truck only gagging and nearly stalling out once before we reached the other closed end of the road. I discovered that by opening my door, leaning out and down, bashing at the pump with my crescent wrench, I could get it working again. This was required more and more often the farther we went. In Creole, a truck mechanic offered to weld a used Peterbilt pump onto the frame. It was about the size of a football. The existing pump was smaller than a fist. A lot smaller. I declined the offer, and we limped up to Lake Charles, me leaning out with the wrench at every stop light.

But, the road, the closed road, was great. Not a single obstruction. Oceanside views. Sea breeze. Our honeymoon tour a decade before any actual nuptials. The whole world our own.

Two months later, Rose started her career as an engineer. I was back in the Tetons, back on the river, when she made her first purchase with her big paychecks. A shiny, hot-off-the-lot, brand-new pickup truck.

Filling out the egg logbook alongside the North Fork at Spruce Creek. (COURTESY OF TOM KOTYNSKI)

Looking across the old Gates Park airstrip from my father's navy hammock.

The inside of the Gates Park cabin, with my bunk and Aidan's Batman pillow.

An evening view from the porch of the Gates Park cabin.

Gates Creek, heading downstream toward the falls.

Approaching the park bridge over the North Fork of the Sun River from the Biggs Flat side.

My boots having a few minutes to dry out while I wear hip boots in Biggs Creek.

The Forest Service cabin at Gates Park in the Bob Marshall Wilderness.

One of many creek crossings, this one over a branch of Headquarters Creek. (COURTESY OF TOM KOTYNSKI)

Bear tracks on top of my own tracks in the trail. (COURTESY OF TOM KOTYNSKI)

The little falls on Gates Creek that keeps the cutthroat trout above it genetically pure.

Heading down from Gates Park to the pack bridge over the North Fork of the Sun River. (COURTESY OF TOM KOTYNSKI)

Adjusting the flow to a Spruce Creek incubator. (COURTESY OF TOM KOTYNSKI)

Listening intently to yet another lecture at the National Park Service law enforcement training.

Nolan, at two, taking the oars on the Missouri River. (COURTESY OF ROSE POWERS)

*Nolan playing,
Montana style.*

*At Bong Recreation
Area waiting to be
released.* (COURTESY
OF DAN FROMM)

Aidan at his usual pace in Utah's Coral Pink Sand Dunes.

16

Bob Marshall Wilderness, Montana
May 2004

I wake, the blackness in the cabin like a fog, the stove wood no longer popping or cracking. The windowpane is a blank, the sky socked in, though I can't hear rain. I click the faint green glow of my watch. Four A.M. Six hours of sleep. In a row. Practically record setting.

A night straight through is something I can barely recall, Nolan, for years the worst sleeper in the history of childhood, shattering our sleep patterns forever, but I try a little longer before sliding my legs over the side of the bunk, my feet down to the cold floor. A day to start by headlamp. But in the quiet this time. Alone. No wardens, no biologists. No boys about to tumble out of their beds.

Lantern. Fire. Coffee. Something to eat, then a little something more, hoping the clouds will lift, the misting rain blow off. After waiting so long in the dark, I make it all the way to eight before, nothing left to do, I head out, the eggs my sole mission.

The water roars beneath the bridge, a full pine tree twisting and turning as it crashes into the bank, bangs the bottom, swings around back into the flow, and I stop halfway across and watch, mesmerized, caught up, as usual, in the rush and flow.

I'd been working in the Tetons nearly two weeks, or, well, if not exactly working, at least trying to learn how to get down the river alive in a raft. Building up experience, I floated after work, before work, on duty, weekends. Pancoast and I paired up as often as we could, each in our own small raft, chasing each other down the river, practicing landing in trickier and trickier spots. We floated through snow, through rain, through brilliant sun, the summer at seven thousand feet opening around us, temperatures climbing, the river-edge snowbanks shrinking, the water rising, turning brown and roiled. Chunks of banks tore loose, disappeared. New channels opened up overnight, and we pushed into openings no wider than our rafts, wanting to be the first to ever float a new route, name it. Then, after scratching our way through flooded trees, dropping over little water falls, we'd pop back out into the rush and tumble of the main channel, get swept off and away downstream. Like cubs, we learned by playing, prepping for the day, should it ever come, that we'd need to be able to land the raft anywhere, under any conditions.

Trees, undercut by the rush, teetered and crashed down. The river filled with a churning chaos of debris, logs, whole trees. Now and then a submerged trunk would strike something beneath the surface and pinwheel, surfacing in a kraken-like slow-motion yaw, its head tilting above the wild water, lifting, streaming, then crashing back down, vanishing. Along the bottom, rocks churned and cracked, the flat rubber of the raft bottom like an eardrum, amplifying the crackling rush and collision of rock and stone, sand and gravel. Popcorn, we called the sound, wondering what would happen if one of those trees suddenly cartwheeled up underneath our rafts.

But it wasn't a surfacing tree that started my first rescue away from Lake Mead, it was one falling, an eighty-foot spruce undercut, losing its grip on the river rock and thin soil. It tilted and then dropped toward the water in almost the same instant, no warning at all for the Lodge Company barge boat loaded with twenty-some passengers drifting directly into its path.

The raft, a thirty-three-footer with tubes three feet in diameter, had originally been a military-bridge platform: float it in, plank it over, drive across the tanks. Too huge to be rowed like a conventional raft, it instead had a sweep at each end, a kind of giant oar the boatmen, one thirty feet away from the other, used in coordination to push the boat one way or another across the current.

When the spruce crashed down, a direct hit across the center of the raft, it somehow managed to miss all the passengers, instead slipping between them to smack down on the tubes, buckling the raft, knocking everyone to the floor, except the two boatmen standing at the far ends of the raft. They were catapulted into the air, each landing near the other's position, jumping up to the other's sweep. But the raft, remarkably unpunctured, straightened back out and continued floating down the river, now carrying the tree as well, its root-ball end dragging the bottom, swinging the raft broadside to the current. The boatmen, with their suddenly puny sweeps, had no chance of controlling anything, and downriver, directly in their path, stood one of the river's largest, most ancient logjams: the Witch's Broom, a decades-old nest of trees and broken timber woven into a nightmare's pick-up-stick collection, all battered and bobbing, gnashing and twisting with the full crush of the river's swollen waters.

As the giant raft and its load of tree and passengers approached the jam, quilled with staubs and splintered trunks, the boatmen told their passengers that they were going to hit, that they were traveling so fast that they wanted all the passengers simply to jump up into the air when they told them to, that their downstream momentum would carry them onto the jam, that if they jumped, they'd clear the face of it, land on top of the logs, be safe there.

And it worked. The boat disintegrated on impact, as if made of tissue paper, the rubber tubing shredding as it was driven into the spikes and barbs of the weathered gray logs. The passengers sprawled and scattered over the top of the jam, scraped and bruised, but dry and safe, if stranded. Only one boatman, controlling his sweep to the last moment, was caught low, a needle-sharp snag tip piercing his leg, driving through between the bone and muscle of his calf. But he too made it to the top of the jam.

We got the call after another boat saw the crew stuck atop the jam, floated down five more miles to Moose

Landing, ran into park headquarters to report what they'd found. Pancoast and I threw our rafts onto a truck, raced the ten miles to Deadman's Landing, rigged our boats, launched, five miles to row to get to the Witch's Broom. Knowing the Broom, my gut twisted, wondering how on earth we'd ever land a boat on it. Still, this was no Lake Mead jolt of sudden adrenaline. For five miles, we shouted plans back and forth across the water, the popcorn chattering at the bottom of our rafts. At best, we'd arrive an hour after the fact. What was done was done. No lives hung in the balance. If we could land, we'd be ferrying the victims safely to shore, to a place they could be reached by car, taken away to their motels and campgrounds. As sick as I was trying to imagine a landing on that pincushion, I couldn't help smiling as we rowed toward it, our rafts like mosquitoes darting across the water compared with the hulk taken out by a tree.

Witch's Broom in sight, we lined up together, back-to-back, Pancoast out front, ferry angles set to pull back into any pocket of broken water as we slid past the people on top of the jam, running the right side of the stretch of logs, the curl of brown water frothing through them. Pancoast found a gap, hauled back on his oars, and just behind him, I found my own. We made it. Landed. Tied off. Jumped out and started to pick our way over the logs to the castaways.

I found the boatman, the only injury, a makeshift bandage already wrapped around his calf. A professional-looking job. I stooped down to inspect, and a passenger, an orthopedic surgeon, assured me it was done right, that I should leave it alone. My smile only grew.

Circling the jam, looking for options, Pancoast and

I decided we could carry our rafts across the top of the jam to the left side, put them down in a channel appearing out of the jam itself, float the passengers out six at a time, down this channel to where it had to hook up with Schwabacher's, take them down that to the old landing there, the same landing I'd been taken out at as a twelve-year-old. Working the radios, we had rangers head there for pickup, an ambulance. More rafts started out from Deadman's.

I took the last load out, a group of tourists hoping only for a quiet, scenic float down before the Tetons, who'd spent hours on the bobbing, shifting jumble of broken trees. Once while we waited, another full-size tree floated down toward the Broom, its root ball jutting at us like the point of a lance. The entire jam shook and lifted at the impact, and, slowly, the top of the tree twisted right, like a pendulum, the whole tree turning down the main channel, pulling off the jam. As it did, the roots caught the inch-thick hemp rope that had been the raft's life line. The rope sprung from the water, tightened instantly to snap point, the water spraying from the tensed fibers as if by some supercharge of electrical current, the air around the rope, in that instant, simply hazed with tiny flying droplets. And then the rope, an inch of woven hemp fibers, snapped as if it were a piece of string. It cracked like a shot, the spray of water gone, the rope gone, the tree twisting off downstream, the jam settling into its regular, rhythmic bob and rustle. The tourists wanted to go home.

And so, as evening fell and I floated them down the little, shallow, peaceful run of Schwabacher's, I tried to calm them, finish their scenic float, leave them with nothing more than an adventure story to tell. I pointed out a beaver lodge, explained its construction, showed them the osprey nest. Drifting perpendicular to the current, I pointed upstream to a heron lifting off, and, all heads turned that way, my downstream oar caught the bottom of the channel, rocketed up through the rubber oarlock, the handle, my fist still wrapped around it, smacking me square in the jaw, clapping my teeth together hard enough to chip enamel, right over my tongue.

I choked back whatever non-rangerly blast I might have let fly, my eyes watering so from the sting and shock that I could barely see, the burn of such a rookie mistake not helping at all. It was a minute or more, the cluster of ranger vehicles visible at last at the landing, my passengers giving a cheer at the sight of them, before one of them turned to me, their rescuer, and saw my chin and shirt stained dark with my blood, the mouthful I couldn't quite swallow back as I rowed, much more carefully, toward the landing.

It was, I think, a less than encouraging sight. But the rescue was done, no mermaid's hair waving beneath the surface, no clawed backs, just a crew of subdued, but smiling tourists, ready to reboot their vacations.

And once they were packed up and driven off, Pancoast and I reloaded our rafts, tied them down on the back of the pickup, and headed north for home. He could not stop laughing about my face, the Elmer Fudd accent mushing around my swollen tongue. I nodded, aching, but kept looking out at those mountains, just purpled flat cutouts of themselves in the gloaming, and felt I'd finally found home.

Bob Marshall Wilderness, Montana
May 2004

Pumping up the hill away from Gates, the exercise fighting off the chill, charged by the water, I can't help but smile. If this daily loop doesn't kill me, it'll make me a titan, the daily workout of tromping in dripping rain gear to peer into unchanged black water in unchanged black buckets.

Without the horses to race, the walk feels slower, or maybe just less directed. I wander off trail, walking down lines of trees, peeking over the backsides of hills. I'm almost surprised to find myself at the creek, sliding down the still-muddy slope, my tracks from yesterday the only ones marring the long grooves of the horses' sliding descent.

If the eggs have changed at all, they've only become less active. But I go through the motions, checking the intakes, the outlets, finding no clogs, no silt, no change. I pull out the log. "Water temp, forty-two, skies overcast, rain intermittent." I feel I'll be writing these words a lot on Dave's waterproof pages.

Nothing else to do but head for Spruce Creek, I climb back to the flats, and as I crest the creek cut, sixty yards ahead of me, something small and black lunges up a tree trunk. I stop dead, the terms "bear" and "cub" rising slowly through the synapses. As black as the burned trees all around it, it shinnies madly up one of the few large, live ponderosas left. "Where's Momma?" I say, and another cub launches itself up the tree, then another. I take a step back, up onto a downed tree, making myself taller, expanding my view, saying, more urgently, "Where's Momma?"

And then there she is, sitting at the base of the tree, her own blackness, broken by the low brush, blending her into the burn. I get off the tree and back up, edging away to the open. As black as they are, I realize, even where I can see a long ways, I won't see the bears. I'll have to sing that much more.

The sow watches me as the two lead cubs keep climbing, maybe sixty feet, while the tail-ender stops, looks at my retreat, then down at Mom, and reverses course, like a lineman coming down a pole, and hits the ground, bounding into its mother's side. She ambles ten yards away from me, the cubs in the tree bawling, but not making a move. The sow moves off farther, and so do I, leaving them as alone and as unthreatened as I can.

I wonder, like the cat perched above the fireman's ladder, if it's as easy for them to make it down, hoping I'll find no broken little bodies at the base.

But the next day, singing wildly, I walk through those

trees, inspecting the ground around the trunk of their ponderosa. Nothing. All safe, all gone. I smile and head down
to my eggs.

Still no need for even a finger swirl, I climb back up
onto the flats, to the trail back north, elk standing everywhere, eyeing me, shuffling off a bit, eyeing me again. Moving into the tight trees before Spruce Creek, I spook a pair of
blue grouse, their heart-stopping flurry of wings blowing
up through the branches all but dropping me dead. I shout
and scream through the rest of the trees, the needled fingers
of the branches brushing at me from both sides, something
that would drive Hansel and Gretel straight to the witch's
cottage. As they blind and deafen me, their rustling in the cold
wind seems nearly threatening, something eerie and spooky
about it, whispery. I clap, stomp, shout, "Hey, Boo-Boo!
Coming through!" on the way back, too.

When, at last, I hit the green clearing of the cabin, I step
out of the cleft of the horse trail and cut across the grass
down to the cabin, circling it, opening shutters, dropping my
pack, kicking out of my boots. The robin and I scare the
daylights out of each other. Home again, home again, rig-
gedy jig.

Inside the silence wraps round me, the stillness, the absence of the boys, and I walk out to the runway with the elk,
veering down to the creek, walking along it to the food
cache, then back up the hill to the cabin, circling my territory as dusk closes in. Inside, I go through the motions: fire,
dinner, book. Just before I have to light the lantern, I slip
Aidan's Batman pillow out of the box beneath my bunk,
sneak one sad-eyed peek at Nolan's napkin, and lie down,

pull my sleeping bag up. I stare out the window, the quarter moon already up and down, the stars beginning to run rampant.

Day after day for the next week the routine changes little. A bear, at distance, here and there, elk everywhere, whitetails around the cabin, the rain incessant, as if I truly do live inside my very own cloud, noons hardly brighter than dawn or dusk. Slopping through another egg patrol, I crack myself up remembering an old hitchhiking standby, belted out on countless stretches of abandoned and empty highways, Gordon Lightfoot's "In the Early Morning Rain." "I'm a long way from home, lord I miss my loved ones so." I add it to my bear-scaring repertoire of bedtime songs.

Home and changed, dry, I stare out the window at the gray and drizzly world, wondering how on earth I would have entertained the boys through this. Eventually I pull the closet box out from under my bed, the casters squealing, the plywood grating against the cross brace at the foot of the bed. Pushing aside my clothes, I retrieve the bag of deer hides I'd set aside for moccasins, the tracings I'd remembered to take of their feet. I use the same booklet of Native American moccasin design that I'd used in Indian Creek, the same pattern even, and roll out a hide, tracing out miniature duplicates of my long-legged Flathead moccs.

Just beginning to turn the tracings of their feet into patterns, I realize I'd forgotten to measure the circumference of their feet. All this leather, all this time, the outline of their feet staring up at me from my sketch-pad paper, so petite compared with my canal boats, and I'd forgotten one vital measurement. Then I notice the pencil notes in the margin of the booklet, my own measurements from twenty-five years before.

I study the scrawled pencil numbers. Maybe a ratio, length of my foot, over circumference, versus their length over x. Grade school math to the rescue. Without any real idea if it'll work, only the hope I don't come home with footwear they can't wedge their feet into with a battering ram, I start to cut. To sew.

I can't return empty-handed.

I shuffle through the egg runs in full rain gear: hood up, head down, slipping and sliding in the mud, singing in the dark parts, trip-trapping over the bridge, bellowing through the Hansel and Gretel stretch of nightmare-close trees.

The trip down the mud and ash bluff to the Spruce Creek eggs is thrill-ride stuff, the mud so much like grease I always wonder how I'll make it back up. But, once down at the incubators, I pull out the cheater glasses I'd only last year been forced to put in my fishing vest for knot tying, and only now have remembered to bring with me, give these eggs a real inspection. As kids we teased our father unmercifully about his thinning hair, his failing near vision, offering to hold the paper across the room for him. It doesn't seem that comical now.

But, up close and in focus, I see change in the observation basket. Dark pink lines, like a streak of blood, curl around the eggs. Spines. No longer just eyes, these eggs have backbone. I sit back and smile. "Well, check you guys out. Fricking vertebrates!"

Otherwise, things are the same as ever, no silt, no need to change water flows or do anything at all. So I claw my way back up the hill, pulling at every log and rock I can reach, then slog on toward Biggs, covered with soot and mud. The sun actually appears for a brief flash, and I dare to take off my rain jacket.

At the northernmost reach of Biggs Flat, looking off into the main spine of the Rockies to the west, the clouds lift high enough that I catch a glimpse of the Chinese Wall, a twenty-mile-long, thousand-foot-high cliff, probably the wilderness's most famous landmark, something I'd always wanted to see. Hidden until now, it stands out clear, sun glinting on its new snow. I stand grinning like some walleyed, groping cave creature just discovering light.

Starting into the big open stretch of the flats, I catch a movement at the edge of the burned timber: another black bear edging along the snags, snuffing around downed logs, pushing on one, moving along. It looks like the sow I'd seen earlier, but without cubs. Sitting up another tree, bawling for Mom?

I watch until it's nearly out of sight, heading north, then stand and continue south. Though I'm in plain sight, we're three hundred yards apart and the wind is not in the bear's favor. If it did see me, I didn't make much of an impression.

Not ten minutes later, on the golf-course-green hills of the far side of Biggs Creek, I see another blob of black. All the burns make black stand out less than normally, but on this open emerald expanse, nothing could have been more naked than this jet-black spot. I stop, and the spot breaks into a lope, a bear at a dead run. It gallops north across the plain, something ass-over-teakettle about it, a black beach ball bounding across green shores. Tumbling straight for the drop into the creek cut, the bear doesn't slow until it dives into the cover of the timber, and maybe not then.

I stand in the grass, my trail leading to the same cut the bear disappeared into. "Seriously?" I say. In my life in the wilds before this, I've seen maybe four bears, and I shake my head, look up and down the stretch of Biggs Creek. I start my descent, bellowing the national anthem. Entering the bucket's dark pocket of timber, I wind up, "and the home of the brave," and scream, "Play ball!" It's not impossible to feel ridiculous.

I clear silt from a few buckets but can't really say if it's new or old. The eggs in the observation baskets, though still less active than when we'd brought them in, twitch now and then, nearly all of them sporting their new spines.

I enter the observations in my log and sit in a gap of sun for a break, saving an apple for the Flats, where I can savor it without panting from the climb up.

At the cabin, the aloneness slams less and less every day. The robin and I get to know each other, and I warn her before dropping my pack on the porch, stand back and wait for her to launch out to a fence post and sit watching while I work my key in and push open the door, breathing in the stillness. Such a rare treat at home, being alone is something I've had to get used to again.

I walk out to the airstrip. A clot of elk lies bedded down

at the far northern end, a few sentinels up on their feet. Leaving them be, I duck into the trees, circling back to the cabin.

Lee had pointed out the solar shower bag, and, despite the distinct lack of solar power, I'd filled it and left it on the porch in the morning. I test it now, surprised by a temperature maybe exceeding lukewarm.

Feeling pretty prissy—a shower after only a week—I traipse buck naked to the root cellar, my shower bag dangling from one hand, towel, soap, and fresh clothes in the other. A pulley mounted at the end of the root cellar's roof serves as the stall, and I hoist the bag up, open the little nozzle, and stand under the dribble and start scrubbing as if it's a race. At a breezy fifty-two degrees, I dry off as if trying to peel skin, dash back into my clothes, and climb onto the sagebrush flat around the cabin. A whole new world.

After dinner I sit listening to the silence, a quiet unbroken by rainfall. I rock back in my chair, smiling, and a wail not quite coyote drifts across the evening air. Something eerie enough I push my chair back, walk to the door, and stand in the last of the sun.

A moment later, another long, lonely, drawn-out howl, somehow mournful. Though I've never heard one before, I grin, whisper, "Wolf." The elk on the runway stand with heads lifted, bodies tensed. At the second howl, they line up, single file, ready to bolt.

Having warmed up, the wolves cut loose, some directly up the hill behind the elk, and another group off to the south toward Red Shale Creek.

Oddly, as the wolves crank up, howling without any of

the yelping or giddy laughing of coyotes, the elk seem to relax, eventually going back to their feeding. Can they understand?

For the ten minutes the wolves speak, I can't stop the tingle along the nape of my neck, or close my mouth, stop my grin.

But they stop as suddenly as they started, and I gradually notice the faint buzz of some late hatch of insects, the darting whir of the swallows feeding on them, zipping in and out of their nests beneath the cabin eaves. In a burned snag across the airstrip, a pair of ravens call to each other with their burbling croak. Everybody celebrating a little sun.

Behind them the clouds race over the mountains, pinking up for a few minutes, then going flat and white, finally darkening to gray with the dusk. Despite their speed, not a breath of wind stirs the meadow, and when I turn back to the cabin, the chimney's wisp of smoke drifts arrow-straight to the sky, the very picture of shelter, or comfort, even home.

The sky goes blue-black, aglow over the mountains. A few planets shine. From the gathering darkness all around me, the sky fills with the odd, whirring, winnowing of snipe.

As a ranger in the Tetons, I'd played softball in the evenings at a field in Moran. Kind of a field anyway—a patch of sagebrush graded down to old river rock and grit. Standing in the weedy expanse of centerfield, the sagebrush behind me waiting to reclaim their ground, I'd listen to the snipe diving, proclaiming their territory with the whistle of wind through spread tail feathers—a hollow, rapid, rising hooing, like a cranked-up mourning dove. Glancing in toward the batter now and then, I'd try to pinpoint the bird by sound, then by eye, occasionally able to spot one of the tiny, diving bodies, the swoop back into the sky, then, a moment later, the sound falling down to me. More often than I cared to admit, my jump on the ball started only at the crack of the bat, my head snapping from the sky back to the game.

Near the end of my first season in the park, in an unusually graceful and athletic play trying to beat out a grounder, I tripped over the first baseman and separated my shoulder. Sage, our pitcher, a seasonal ranger of twenty-some seasons, ran up to me, saw the collarbone straining against the skin over the top of my shoulder, and, though he barely knew me, guessed some twenty-two-year-old first-year ranger would have no health insurance, and said, "Kid, you tough it out until morning; then you fall off the truck tying down your raft." I smiled, nodded—an insured, work-related injury—and he said, "Now get out of here. You never played tonight."

But it was too late. The boss lived across the road from the field, had seen the commotion from his front window, ran across to the game he never joined in on, and declared that this was an off-duty injury, that he'd witnessed it, that he, the park, was not responsible. He did, however, offer to drive me down to the hospital in Jackson. He took his cruiser, me wincing and gasping at every bump, every corner, holding on to my elbow, pushing my arm up, keeping the collarbone under the skin. He punched his radar button on the way down, caught a speeder, left me sitting in the back while he did his traffic stop, wrote out the ticket.

The following surgery knocked me off the oars of my river patrolman's duties, and on my first day back from the hospital, Sage (his lesser-used name was Bob DeGroot—even his official uniform name tag read merely SAGEBRUSH) greeted me at the ranger station, pointed at my sling, my arm, and said, "Well, kid, looks like you'll be riding with me." It was like being invited behind the wizard's curtain. A World War II vet, onetime world record holder in the hundred-yard backstroke, Sage had worked in the Tetons for so long that nobody really had any clear idea of what it was he actually did. The park enigma, this sixty-something guy who looked forty, still a swimmer's build, a head full of blond hair, piercing-blue eyes, and an always ready grin, showed up at my house every morning, switched his truck for the government truck, said hello when he came in to take his key off the rack by the door, and then drove off, often not to be seen or heard from again until he pulled back in that evening, dropped off the government truck, and drove off to his home up Pacific Creek.

I climbed into his truck beside him, numbed by painkillers but prickly with curiosity. What Sage actually did, I discovered, was explore. Everything, everywhere, all the time, not bothering with districts or boundaries or much of anything else. On my birthday, a month after I almost made it to first, he drove us miles outside the park toward Togwotee Pass. I wondered, aloud, what we'd do if something came up in the park, something we were needed for. He answered by flicking off the park radio. "They've got plenty of people working down there."

He turned onto a dirt road, driving up and up until we hit snow. We got out, turned in the hubs, continued on, slithering through growing drifts, the road progressively primitive. "Sage," I said, "what if we get stuck way the hell out here?"

The front tires bounded up, clawing at snow, failing to reach through to the gravel. High-centered. I told myself, *I told you so*.

Sage spun the wheels a second, satisfied, then twisted the key, killing the engine. Turning to me in the new quiet, he said, "Kid, what you've got to learn is to relax. That's what I'm trying to teach you here." He reached into the backseat of the big green Dodge, retrieving a six-pack. He set it between us on the front seat. "Happy birthday, kid!" he said, prying off a couple of caps, clicking the glass of his longneck against mine.

We stayed until the six-pack was gone, then got out and dug ourselves free. I wanted him to be my mentor for life.

Leaving the snipe, my breath leaving clouds I can barely make out in the dark, I give a shiver and turn back into the cabin. Not bothering with the lantern, I strip down and slide under my sleeping bag, easing my head down on Aidan's pillow. Through the window, I see that the robin has settled in too, its head poking above one side of the nest, its tail the other. In the wild skies beyond it, even in the dark, the snipe keep up their rising and falling, telling everyone what's theirs.

18

Bob Marshall Wilderness, Montana
May 2004

The next morning, instead of slop and rain, I kick through frost on my way out of the park, the sky clear, the sun climbing above the mountains as I slip down the stiff mud to the river at Spruce Creek and back into shadows. There, in the crystal-clear number 4 bucket, I discover a single egg with a tail. Like a tiny, pink tadpole, it swims away from me, or the light, burrowing in under the other, slower, eggs. In number 5, there are more, and in a few of those I can see ribs along with the spines, and maybe even gills, some kind of rapid, rhythmic respiration. As the sun reaches even here, I tip to block it from the delicate DNA, can't quite stop a proud, parental smile. These kids are going places. I jog up the slope, hustle down to Biggs, but the eggs there are, well, still just eggs.

But, with even just the idea of sunshine, I've carried my fly rod all the way, waving it like a baton as I marched across the flat, and I break down Biggs for the North Fork, maybe a mile downstream.

For a long way, Biggs Creek looks like something you might find in LA, an almost straight shot of featureless river rock, no cover, no vegetation, no holding water. A waterway or canal more than a mountain stream. I wonder how the grayling, three-eighths of an inch long, will do tumbling down this raceway.

Then the hills tighten to the creek, the brush and trees too, and soon I'm crawling down deer trails through thickets of unburned timber, scrambling over deadfall. Visibility drops to a few yards, and, with the creek rushing, the wind chuffing through the leaves and needles, I can barely hear myself as I try to sing and shout. I start to wonder if I'm on a deer trail, or bear. If I get devoured on my way to go fishing, Rose will pick through the bear shit just to stomp on my remains.

Eventually the bluffs open into a wide flat, the creek braiding into a delta on its last run to the river, the opposite shore a steep cliff only a few hundred yards away through the grass and river rock, what's left, after the fires, of a large stand of big cottonwoods. Only a step into the clearing I stumble across an enormous load of ancient bear shit, all hair and bone fragments, uniformly crumbly and weathered the lifeless gray of old man's hair. I glance behind at the trail I've just emerged from. Shifting some jerky strips out of their Ziploc, I bag the two biggest turds. Backwoods treasure for the boys.

Last year's dead, gold grass sweeps my legs until I reach the cutbank at the water's edge. Almost clear, the river races by, more water than I'd pictured while sitting at home. Big water really, though the bank of white river rock I stand on shows that at times it's much bigger yet.

I set up my rod and fish the hole beneath the creek junction without success. It feels so good to be in the sun, I couldn't care less, and I walk downstream, casting as I go.

Not half a mile down, the channel splits around an island, my side hooking sharply into a cliff face I could climb, maybe find a way back down on the other side, but, given the pace of the fishing, it seems like an overdose of effort and optimism both.

Instead, I take off my pack, dig out the water bottle and a bratwurst I'd cooked the day before, and lie down in the grass. The taste is the same I've known since backyard Wisconsin barbecues, and I see perfectly the cracked and patched asphalt of our driveway, the rectangle of strike zone I'd scratched onto the white garage door with a clod of dirt, spending hour after hour practicing my pitching, whacking a tennis ball against the garage door, something that must have, for years, created a mind-numbing, repetitive boom inside, something my mother never once complained about.

Bracketed by the waving grass, a series of brilliant white clouds drifting west, deepening the blue, I close my eyes, let the sun redden the black behind my eyelids. When I wake, I push up and start upstream, but that way, beyond Biggs, the entire river is closed off by cliffs, cutting off my hope to follow it home. So I turn into the burned hills, huffing through the downed timber, finding every tree that's just an inch too high to step over before finally reaching the flats, lupine scattered everywhere, bluer than the sky.

The miles pile on, the sun relentless, something, after all the rain, I start to have to remember to enjoy. At the last little creek crossing I finish off my water, eyeballing the trail's only long, steep hill, a dusty south-facing switchback broiling in the sun. I do a fake shiver, and boom out, "The Hill of Doom!" a game I'd played with the boys, sitting on the lip of the little slope in our front yard, flipping them over my back as they tried to push me down.

Even a hot, dusty hill in the middle of nowhere leads straight to them. Pushing myself up, my breath coming in regular rasping pants, I wonder if in my old age I'll be unable to cross a room of our house without drawing up pictures of them as children. I kind of hope so.

At the top of the hill I stop at the small, reed-filled pond beside the trail, and, finding a suitable throwing stone, I skip the windup and go straight from the stretch, pitching the rock at a reed clump in the pond's center, missing by about four feet. I bark, "Ball!"

Climbing the hill on the Gates side of the pack bridge, entering the dark timber above the falls, I can hardly not follow "Fox Went Out on a Chilly Night" with "Take Me Out to the Ball Game," the order Nolan demanded for years. I used to skip verses sometimes, to get it over with faster. What on earth had I been thinking?

I get home and soak my head in the creek, peel into shorts, a non-sweat-soaked T-shirt, swap my boots for sandals. Then, revived, I open up the bunkhouse, yanking my father's old navy hammock out of the Duluth pack. I lug the heavy canvas sheet out to the edge of the airstrip and stretch it between two likely-looking trees.

As kids we'd all spent time in this hammock, hardly pay-ing attention to the black letters stenciled across the white canvas: D. F. FROMM RT 3/C 306-70-84. Radio technician, third class. I don't know what the numbers signify. There's a story my dad likes to tell: me in trouble for something, him chasing me down for a little bit of a sit-down, but me getting the hammock between us, him caught, beat, picturing the two of us in a Brer Rabbit rundown around the trees, trying hard not to laugh.

A few years ago, I'd been back in Wisconsin visiting when my parents asked if there was any of their camping gear I thought I could use. In their seventies, they'd decided their sleeping-on-the-ground days were in their past. The old Duluth pack came to mind, and they added their tent. I thought a moment more and asked about the hammock.

My dad blanched, and I tried to take back my request. He admitted to not being sure, to thinking he might not want to let it go. My mom said something about not having used it in years. "Why would we want it?" she asked. But my dad, seeming self-conscious, couldn't give in. My parents had, as far as I knew, never been close to sentimental, but that did not lessen my embarrassment over having asked.

A week or so after that, back in Montana, a package arrived, the hammock carefully folded and boxed, a note from my dad saying he'd surprised himself and knew he would never use it again and would be glad if the boys got any use out of it. He didn't know what he'd been thinking.

I place the Batman pillow on the canvas and ease in. I gaze across the long meadow of the airstrip, the breeze eddying over me. The rolls of moccasin pieces I didn't know would even fit sit untouched in my lap. I know what he was thinking. So much gets away from us. And the boys have used the hammock, every year, as crazy for it as we had been.

Eventually, I open up the leather, start sewing, finish the feet, stitch on the tall, wraparound uppers. Lying on my back, my filet knife stuck into a block of wood pinched between my knees, I run a scrap of leather round and round against the blade, cutting five feet of laces. When I finish, I pull the moccasin over the bit of kindling, wrap the top, the laces, tie them shut. Aidan at long last able to dress to his inner savage.

Elk wander onto the runway as I work, one coming straight in to the salt block by the corral, not giving me a second glance. Another comes from behind, passing at the edge of the sage, twenty yards away. The wind blows toward me, and though I'm in plain sight, none of the elk pay the slightest attention. Maybe, as a horizontal thing suspended between two trees, no head, no legs, no connection to the ground, I'm simply not a threat, about as unhuman as it's possible to get.

As I watch this second elk move in to the salt, get half-heartedly chased off by the first, a coyote ducks under the buck rail across the runway, gives a glance up and down the open strip, then trots out, head down, searching for ground squirrels.

The group of elk at the far end of the runway stop grazing, keep their eyes on the coyote. They don't, however, look as ready to bolt as the night the wolves howled. In fact, they look as aggressive as a bunch of cow elk can look, taking a few steps toward the coyote, who keeps his eyes just as carefully on them.

A pair of cows break from the group, making a dash at the coyote. He jumps sideways, skittering off a ways, and the elk slow. But as soon as the coyote stops, they start after him again. He keeps sidling away, stopping, and they keep after him, like songbirds after a hawk. Finally the elk break into a real gallop, chasing the coyote until he tucks his tail low and tears out underneath the buck rail, not stopping to look behind until he's safely at the edge of the trees. Even then he only halts a moment before turning and disappearing into the timber.

I take my chance during the distraction to roll out of the hammock, sneak back toward the cabin, but only make it halfway there before a long, drawn-out, grunting whistle bellows out from the hill behind the cabin. The elk bugles again, nothing I expected to hear in the spring. The elk on the runway lift their heads, offering a few yelps and half bugles in return. The bull on the hill gives another full screaming answer, and I find him, picked out by the last of the sun, tawny-brown on the green hillside, already a six point, the antlers thick in velvet. He dips his head back, gives a shorter bugle, followed by three or four throaty grunts. I can't help but smile.

Moccasins rolled under my arm, I start again for the cabin, when in the long-grass meadow to the south I spot four whitetails eyeing a coyote mousing nearby. Using the same strategy they do in snow, the coyote hunches up, feet close together, head cocked to the side, listening. Then it jumps into the air, coming down stiff-legged, its front feet together, dropping its snout to see if it has actually pinned a mouse to the ground underneath all that grass.

At its first pounce, the deer leap skittishly away, and the coyote, mouseless, lifts its head toward the crowd of bouncing white flags, looking as if it can't quite understand what all *that*'s about. Then it returns its attention to the grass, tilting its head. A minute or so later, it pounces again. This time it comes up tossing its head back, a mouse pitching into the air, caught an instant later. Like kids lobbing up popcorn. Down the hatch. The coyote moves forward a few yards and stops to listen.

It seems I am not the only one enlivened by the reappearance of the sun.

I stay out until after it drops below the mountains, and a half hour later the moon comes up, almost full. A cold night ahead.

Leaving the stove unstoked, I slip beneath my sleeping bag, click off my headlamp. The moon lights up the whole meadow outside my window, the grass silvery gray. The whitetails graze only yards from the porch. At home, they're all asleep.

19

In the Tetons I slept on the top floor of an old log cabin, an original homesteader's place: logs a foot in diameter stained dark with woodsmoke and time, the stone fireplace and its enormous chimney studded with blocks of petrified wood. The sun slipped into my bedroom through the window at the peak of the gabled end, winding through the antlers of the elk skull pinned to the ridge log. In the roof, between the ceiling boards and the roof sheathing, the bats streamed out every evening, poured back in every morning, a scrabbling, scratchy, runway crawl. Just as I do at Gates, I left the window open always. Bugling elk, chattering coyotes, burbling ravens—all of it in there with me. Some mornings I could see my breath.

And those mornings—the early shifts, the only one moving in the world, sliding a raft off the back of the truck as quietly as I could just to hold on to the silence. The river, hidden by the last fogs of night, hustled past, its whisperings and murmurings only deepening the silence. I pushed off into the wreathing mists, shivering, hardly daring to breathe, afraid I'd break some spell I didn't even understand.

Hours later, the sun would clear the mountains, burning everything open, the river no longer shrouded but glinting and shifting and shadowed, more alive than anything in the world. Eventually, the first visitor boats appeared: tourists and fishing guides and the big, lumbering rafts of the scenic floats. And though I'd had the river to myself all those hours, I always wanted more, slipping into side channels no one else knew about, avoiding the visitor contacts I was paid for, not something I could help.

We all knew the eagle nests, and some of us the ospreys', fewer the beaver dens, the otters'. I found a bluebird's nest I could peek into while floating by, check on the progress within. Day after day after day we floated. If a snag shifted position, or a leaning tree collapsed, we'd note the change the next day, the same way, I suppose, a person walking down a city street on their way to work might notice if a building happened to vanish overnight.

Once, caught in a storm, one I saw coming, was able to pull off for, I flipped the boat over me like an awning, but then had to hold on to it as the wind fought to kite it away. The rain thundered over, smothering, and then began to bounce, quarter inch hail hammering in so intensely that in minutes the ground was covered, then glazed smooth, drifts of ice piling up, milky in the sun that followed on its heels, the squall racing off upstream.

Other times, I'd ship the oars and lie back in the sun, feet up over the shafts, hands clasped like a pillow behind my head. The aspen fluttered on the hillsides, the cottonwoods along the banks, and I could imagine no place in the world I would rather be. None. Not even close. Even with the hail pounding down.

Sage came down the river with me now and then, taught me the trick of pulling the cross tubes out of our little patrol rafts, pulling the sleeping bag out of our rescue gear, showed how the whole raft could be turned into a water bed. "You have yourself a hard night, just pull into one of those little side channels of yours, tie up, and you catch up on your rest." Sleepy Time Channel was born not long after.

On full-moon nights I'd float the Snake again, a route that I knew well enough to feel my way down in the cloud-covered stretches and that in full moonlight sparkled muted, silvered rather than bright, the river running molten, like mercury, a place reborn, remade. What on earth did other people live for?

Off the river, whole rides back upstream in the traffic disappeared without a trace. Even if I was driving. I'd pull into the river cache, start hauling out the rafts to clean, the gear to put away, and only then realize, still mesmerized by the river, that I had no recollection of the drive, could not really say how I'd gotten here.

During the late-fall elk-hunt season, the river shut down by snow and ice, I'd drive poacher patrols all night, the park again zeroed down to all but me. I'd cruise empty roads beneath blankets of stars, park where radio reception was strong enough to pull in a few World Series games, sip coffee, and follow the action, the snow on the Tetons aglow in starlight, the river casting the same light back up off its unfrozen riffles.

Back on the water for another season, a flash of yellow sliced beneath my raft, a razor-thin ripple there and gone. I cut toward the bank, pulled upstream in the quieter water, and made a second pass. A line, maybe a fly line. An hour later, soaked and shivering, I pulled the whole fly rod out of the depths. The first of three the river would turn over to me. Suddenly the flies the visitors left freckling the shoreline branches gained importance. From a kayak, on a good day, I could gather in twenty, thirty, fifty flies. I took up fly-fishing, a whole new reason to be lost to waters. A raincoat appeared snagged on a midstream stump. A cooler. Lifejackets. Paddles.

On a Montana river, my gang rounded up in a pair of rafts, another flash caught my eye, deep in the heart of a logjam. I pulled in, clambered across the sticks, and dug out a hat I still wear today. Downstream in the other raft, people wanted to know what I was doing. Rose shook her head. "Shopping," she told them.

My twin brother, an engineer in Rochester, New York, ever since graduating from college, came out to visit, and I took him down rivers, up mountains. Around a campfire, as I burned the broken handle out of a hatchet head and he filled me in on the secrets of tempering metals, the talk turned to our different lives, how he'd taken time off, flew out, how this week was a significant fraction of his year's free time, how he was spending it here doing basically what I did every day. I had, it seemed, time to burn, while he had the money to do whatever he wanted—hell, even buy a new

hatchet instead of ruining the temper on this broken one—
but for only a few weeks a year. My money ran nearly out
every spring, after the months unemployed. No nest-egg
building, no retirement, no 401(k)s, not even any plane tickets. I'd never had a credit card. But we both seemed to have
what we wanted, neither pining for the other's world. Paul
acknowledged mine was pretty sweet but supposed that
later it would be harder. I could do nothing but nod at the
flames, poke at the coals with a stick. Later. Like this curse
out there, the future, waiting. I could really see nothing out
there that would bring it closer.

But years rolled by. Rose moved to Great Falls to start
her own engineering career. My brother got married, visited
less. My parents, so willing to give me my lead years before,
to let me range out alone, now began to wonder, wanting
me to at least try imagining other places I could be. They
talked about life plans, income, full-time employment, asked
what I would be doing in five years, ten, twenty. Asked what
Rose would be doing. Did we talk about marriage? kids?
My grandmother, figuring the only thing that could possibly
be causing all this life to hang fire was my lack of resources,
gave me one of her diamond rings, told me to get the stones
made into a new ring. To Rose she said, "If I were you, I'd
have shown him the gate ages ago."

They were just concerned, afraid I'd been lost to the
world, eddied out, gone missing on the rivers. At twenty,
twenty-five, thirty, I could see no harm in that. But kids.
Could they be a whole new river sweeping me away?

Bob Marshall Wilderness, Montana
May 2004

Lost in the Tetons, adrift on the Snake, for maybe the first time I sleep well enough to loiter in bed, watch the light seep into the day. A bull elk, the biggest I've seen so far, with six solid points of thick velvety antlers, walks past the window. Maybe the bugler from across the creek. He looks to be in much better shape than the cows, his coat gleaned of all traces of winter hair, darker and sleeker. I shift up to an elbow, and he spooks, but only jumps sideways before resuming his grazing.

After letting him feed his way out of sight, I get out of bed, find myself tiptoeing, giving the elk as much peace as possible. I click on the Forest Service radio for the weather report and suddenly remember Tom asking me to check in with Choteau every morning. A welfare check. Letting them know I'm still alive. Dialing the volume down to a whisper, I call in for the first time.

The dispatcher says, "You're *who?*" Apparently my silence hasn't caused too much distress.

I explain who, and where, and what, and the dispatcher says thanks and have a nice day. I smile, tell him to have one, too. A conversation.

I tune to the round-the-clock weather report. A scorcher called for in Great Falls, seventy-five to eighty-five, but here, up in the mountains, sixty-five to seventy. I decide to dare shorts, go early to beat the heat.

I bolt down my oatmeal and dig out my old Park Service uniform shirt for its chest pockets, one side for binos, the other for the notepad Aidan had given me, so I would remember what to tell him. I slide my belt through my shorts, pausing on the left hip for my bear spray, the right for my revolver.

Chilly at first, the hills keep me warm until the sun gets over the mountains. I find elk grouped up in the burns, four here, eight there, and when I reach the north end of Biggs Flat, I run into eighty or so, stretching from the trail all the way to the tops of the green hills to the east, all heading my way. The tail end of the group branches around the burned stand of aspen I drop down in. Out of sight, I wait.

They part around me like water, five cows and yearlings to my right, barely giving me a glance, five on my left, skirting the edge of the burn, thirty yards away, more suspicious. Little noticeable breeze, what there is must be heading their way. They stop and stare, stretching their necks, shifting their weight from foot to foot before finally putting up their noses and trotting past. The five on the right, seeing this, widen the distance between us but keep on, joining up

with the others behind me. Then they put their heads down
to feed.

I stay still, but eventually, no matter how little I want to
disturb them, it's time to move on. I stand up and the group,
like a school of fish, bolt as one, all bunching their muscles,
digging in their hooves and exploding away together. They
shoot forty or fifty yards up the hill and, again as one, stop,
staring at me, not as if they'd watched me carefully only
minutes before, but as if I had suddenly appeared straight
out of the ground.

I only take a couple of steps when the first cow barks.
Five or six more yelps follow. I chuckle all the way to Biggs,
the cows, like playground bullies, talking tough only after
I'm heading away.

Hoping to slow myself down a little, keep the hikes from
turning into death marches, I've brought along the battered
copy of Hemingway's *Nick Adams Stories* I'd picked up in
Samoa on my way back from New Zealand, and after the
check on the eggs I climb back onto the flats and walk to a
huge Doug fir just off the trail, one of only a few left from
the fires, perfectly shaped for shade.

Elk tracks print the dust-dry dirt beneath the tree, dirt so
fine I can make out the print of their hair where they'd lain.
I toss aside the few stones and pinecones and sit down. From
beneath the branches, I have a long view down the flats to
the burned woods where I'd seen the black bear ambling
along and, turning slightly to the left, to where the cubs had
launched up their tree.

Settling in against the trunk, I slip *Nick* out of my pack,
take a long drink of water, a bite of apple, and read "Indian

Camp," marveling over it, as always. When he wasn't working so hard to live up to his myth, Ernie could really write.

But I take to the reading like the hiking, diving straight
into the next story, forging on. I force myself to close it, to
watch the undulations of the grass, to study a few burned
stumps I try to turn into bears, one long-downed cottonwood, just a few silver logs mostly hidden by grass. It's a
still moment, near the heat of the day, and it seems nothing
moves, only the drone of a few flies, the distant croak of a
raven.

I take one more drink and reload my pack. My sweat-
wet shirt, flattened against my shoulder blades by the
pack, shakes me with a chill.

Just the detour to Spruce left, those dark trees. I start off.

Crossing Headquarters Creek, climbing up out of the
pack bridge's dip, I make the ridgetop trail, the river a silver
wrinkle below me, the latest fires having cleared out this
whole stretch. An osprey glides down the river, too close to
the goose pair whose nest sits high atop a broken snag. They
launch out, chasing the osprey down the river cut, honking
and flapping for all they're worth, one circling back to the
nest, the other in pursuit all the way around the bend, out
of sight. I can't imagine an osprey as much of a threat to their
eggs, their chicks, but still, safety first.

I plod on, getting close to the Hansel and Gretel stretch,
the boogeyman bend, where my entire world condenses to
the few feet around me.

But still out in the open, the hairs on the back of my neck
go up, my shoulders jumping in a shiver. It's hard being
sure what you hear while walking out in the wild, all the

close little noises—the rustle of clothes, the tread of feet against rock and stone, twig and needle, the wind, the water—blocking out others. But, still, I stop dead, turning my head this way and that, straining to hear.

And there it is again, no mistake, what I haven't heard in seventeen years. A roar in the wilderness.

I turn toward it, facing the river, the canyon. On the steep hill of the other side, in the low scrub of new growth, the few blackened points of the snags, they're not hard to pick out. Maybe two hundred yards away, the drop and climb of the river cut putting them nearly at eye level, a pair of grizzlies, one wrestling with something behind a charred log, the other standing back, moving in, then away. Thirty yards above them, a cow elk paces, watching their every move.

The bigger bear, the one behind the log, lifts its head, tugging backward, and the hind leg of an elk calf tilts up, then flops back down. The smaller bear, which seems full-size itself, inches closer while the big bear's head is down, until, without warning, the big grizzly bursts out, hurdling the log, barreling toward the smaller bear, front legs spread wide, hair bristled out, a massive, terrifying rush that steals my breath from across a river. I've heard of men standing still in the face of these charges, waiting for the bear to veer off at the last instant, knowing most are false charges, and I wonder what flows through their veins, or if they simply froze, only later coming up with a theory to explain their failure to move a single muscle. The smaller bear knows what to do, tripping over itself in full-scale retreat.

The big bear—really, it should be the "huge bear" and the "slightly less huge bear"—doesn't bother giving chase.

Instead, another roar drifts across the river to me. The big bear stomps once, then turns back, climbing across the log it had leapt over before, and lowers its head into whatever's left of the calf. The less huge bear circles back in.

Above them, the cow calls to her calf, that plaintive, throaty chirp. Neither bear so much as looks in her direction.

The next time the bigger bear lifts its head, I have my binos out, the red of blood clear on its muzzle. It pulls up strips of something, intestines maybe. The cow calls.

The other bear shifts left, then right, circling, minutes passing, always a little closer, until the big bear charges again, little more than five yards, one heart-stopping lunge. The smaller bear stumbles back maybe twice that far, stands watching, shifting its head left, then right, not quite looking at the other bear. The big bear stares bloody-faced, eyeing the smaller, and from above, ignored, the cow moves down the hill, closer to her calf, as if there were still something she could do, something she could save.

The big bear swings its head around to watch her. The cow keeps coming, moving gingerly, lifting a foot forward, reaching, then pulling it back, then forward again, touching the ground, then lifting her foot back up, like a cat testing the water. She calls, and the bear watches, letting her get a few steps closer before breaking out in yet another charge, up the hill toward her, three, maybe four lunges, covering ten or fifteen yards in an instant. The cow skitters back, but no farther than she'd originally been. She calls.

The big bear turns, ambles back down behind the black log, lowers its head. Its shoulders bunch as it pulls at something. Its head rears back, jaws opening, closing. The smaller bear circles in, watching, unable to move closer, unable to give up.

The cow calls.

I watch for maybe twenty minutes, lying down behind the ridge crest, hidden. The action repeats itself like an endless loop, the bigger bear pushing away the smaller, then the cow, then feeding, then starting all over.

Spruce Creek isn't far off, and I decide to get down there and back before this pair is done, while I still know where they are. I stand up, in plain sight, and hustle down the trail, peeking over my shoulder again and again, though the bears never appear to glance my way. I disappear into the thick trees, long black claws and gleaming white teeth bristling behind every branch. I shout, "Out of my way!" and breathe again when I'm in the clear on the other side, Red Riding Hood safe at Grandma's. I rush down the slope to the eggs, nearly in free-fall, just enough of a bend in the river to hide the bears up on the opposite hill, that sad, lonely cow.

After a quick, routine check on the grayling, I climb back up and reach the dark stretch, this time closing in on the bears. No matter how I rush, though, I don't guess there's enough of a calf elk to hold them as long as I've been gone. I clap and shout my way through, and when I get back to where the calf had been killed, I pick apart the entire hillside with my binoculars. Not one animal: no bear, no elk, no calf.

By the time I make it back to the cabin I'm hoarse from singing, from shouting. Hoarse, and anxious, and thrilled.

The only other time I've heard that roar, my first real run-in with a grizzly, had been years after Indian Creek, my last year in the Tetons.

The border at the northern reaches of the park, the postcard-perfect mountains away to the south and west, the Snake winding in front of them like a photo op, was rough, steep country, dog-haired with lodgepole, mostly unvisited, and almost totally unmarked. The minds down at HQ, puzzling over anything to puzzle over, like Gags's supervisors in Helena, began to worry about hunters infiltrating from the Teton Wilderness to the north and decided that I, having worked on the river for six seasons, was the perfect choice to delineate this riverless, pathless line on a map.

So Pancoast ferried me to the boundary, cannonballing the old Dodge up the wilderness road, the cottonwoods along Pacific Creek flashing past, tinged yellow by frost, the aspen flaring gold in sheltered pockets amid the heavy greens of the spruce and pine blanketing the mountains. Top speed his only speed, he hockey-stopped in front of the wilderness boundary sign at the end of the road, our dust plume coiling through the open windows. I folded out the free park-visitor map and we studied it one last time. "So, goes north for a while," I murmured. "Then straight west, with that one little jog. Looks, what? Five miles? Six?"

"Close enough," Pancoast said. "You bring a compass?"

I patted my pocket.

"Be like falling off a log."

I waved toward the scruff of lodgepole hiding the pick-up-stick deadfall underneath.

Pancoast smiled. "Like falling off a log, over one, under one . . ."

"Have you ever even been up here before?"

He laughed. We were river men. Fools for water. "There's not even a pond up there," he said. No fishing. Nothing. "You bring water?"

"Just a bottle." In the days before anyone ever talked about giardia, we always camped at water, drank straight from creek or river or lake. Not a possibility up here. "I think I'll just haul for Pilgrim Creek."

He raised an eyebrow. It wasn't early, and my pack held hundreds of the foot-long, three-inch-wide plastic signs, white blazed green with the buffalo and arrowhead. GRAND TETON NATIONAL PARK BOUNDARY. I was assigned to wire one up to every tree I saw, picket-fence style. This would not be straight-ahead backpacking.

I hauled my pack out of the truck bed, threw it onto my shoulder with a groan. The rolls of bailing wire, the fencing hammer, hatchet, and water. Service revolver. Not straight-ahead backpacking at all. I said, "North, west, the one jog."

"A sign every other tree or so," he said, the boss's instructions. Up here, I'd be out of signs in a few hundred yards.

Pointing at the fly rod wrapped inside my sleeping pad and poncho, he said, "What're you planning on fishing for? Grizzlies?"

"In case I make Pilgrim Creek."

"Dreaming," he said. "See you tomorrow. The dump road. What time?"

Six miles, as the crow flies, walking a straight line through impossibly unstraight country, wiring signs all along the way. "Hell if I know," I said.

Pancoast nodded. "I'll bring a book." He slammed his door and leaned out the window. "Remember, the fate of the National Park Service rests with you!"

I started uphill.

I sweated and groaned the rest of that day, trying to follow the old boundary signs when I could, a very sparsely dotted line of antique metal placards, wiring my plastic signs at least within sight of the last one, the bundles of them diminishing more quickly than the miles. As afternoon crawled toward evening, my water bottle long emptied, not a scrap of clear ground flat enough or long enough to stretch out in, my nebulous plans to make it all the way through to Pilgrim Creek grew more solid. Water, a creek-side camp spot, some fish, maybe, for dinner would sure beat crunching up against a tree trunk all night.

As dusk closed in, early with the building overcast, I finally came to the cut of Pilgrim Creek. My non-topo map simply showed a straggling blue line, the same one I could see from the top of the cliff I stood on. I swung upstream, looking for a gap, then down, until I found a break, a chute of sorts, a gravel pitch steep enough I could keep one hand on the hill behind me as I snowplowed down hundreds of feet, ending up in a pile at the bottom. Across the creek, the canyon wall rose just as steeply, but by sheer luck I'd found the lone flat spot, a cobble beach scraggled over with willow and chokecherry, even a stand of lodgepole crowded between cliff and water, a few big, old, dark spruce, their lower branches sweeping the ground.

The slice of sky I could see lowered and darkened as I strung a line between a downed spruce snag and its broken stump, hung my poncho over it, tacked down the corner with sticks I whittled with my hatchet, drove in with the flat backside. I slipped my pad and old down bag underneath.

Living a decade on the wages of a seasonal ranger, my camp gear was more under-the-bridge than REI. No tent, no stove, no freeze-drieds. Not even a flashlight, let alone one of the bitching new headlamps. Just a heavy, Vietnam-era, rubberized poncho, a quarter-inch-thick foam pad, hardened and cracked with age. For cooking I had a four-inch-wide piece of old stove grill, the leftover of what I'd cut down to fit inside my woodstove at Indian Creek, and a charred black one-pound coffee can with a loop of coat hanger as a handle. The menu was a bag of rice (dinner) and a bag of oatmeal (breakfast). A few years before, Rose, spoiling me rotten, had expanded my horizons by introducing me to a bouillon cube.

I set my pack against the spruce with the thickest, lowest branches, the wind rustling down the creek tinged with the scent of rain. I broke off handfuls of the lodgepole's dead, dry lower twigs, scavenged for driftwood, fallen branches, building up a stock that would carry me through the night's cooking, a few hours curled around the flames reading, enough for a small boil for the oatmeal in the morning.

Just before last light, I set up my fly rod. The creek was small, and low, but I cast to a hole the size of my backpack and brought up a brookie on the first cast. Two more followed, just enough for dinner, just before dark. I squatted where I'd cast, slid in the blade of my Swiss Army knife, and tossed the guts into the fastest line of water downstream, a treat for the otters, or mink, or skunk, whatever was lucky enough to make the first stroll through here.

There was, then, very little of the bear-aware mania there is now. At least not in the Tetons. Yellowstone was grizzly country, Glacier, but the grizzlies were only just beginning to wander south. I'd cut tracks while bushwhacking north of here, had found hair, scratch trees, but never really gave them much thought. If a lake showed tracks, I'd fish and cook in one spot, then camp on the other side. That was about it. On this gravelly spit, a bear would have to work awfully hard to leave a track, and eating and sleeping in different spots was an option only for an osprey. This was *the* spot. I didn't think any of this through at the time.

Instead, I built up a little fire, grilled my fish, boiled my rice and bouillon cube, and ate by the light of the flames. After dinner, I pulled on a wool shirt and opened my book, the cold coming up off the creek, breezing through the upstream pines, fanning the dying flames, rustling the needles and leaves against one another. As I read about Doc and the boys in Cannery Row, I added more wood than I'd counted on, scooched a little closer to the fire. Gathering more in the morning would not be a problem.

Then, one rustle was different than all the others. I lifted my head, peered upstream, upwind, over the flames. Nothing there beyond the touch of firelight on the first row of needles and branches but the dead black of a low night. I turned my head, straining to hear. Nothing but wind, trees, the creek.

I had spent more nights out like this than I could count. I knew a squirrel flitting across a camp could sound like a rhino. And a chuffing, stomping muley buck? Good god. T. rex.

I went back to my reading.

A crack of something, not just a twig snap, but something bigger, bent, then breaking. I forgot to close my thumb between the pages. I put Steinbeck down and rubbed at the back of my neck, the shiver there. I studied the few dimly lit branches, turned my head first one way, then the other, listening.

I put a few small branches on the fire, sticks that would flare up.

A twig cracked. Then another. Footsteps, nothing else. Something walking out there.

I gathered my feet under me. Put a knee down, a hand. A runner in the blocks. A sprinter with no place to dash.

"Hello?" I said.

The steps stopped. Just the wind again, the creek. I listened for minutes. Eased back down a bit. I started to smile, shake my head. Spooked by nothing. I poked the fire up, put in another branch, just the end, in case I needed a torch, something I'd tried before, which never worked like in the movies. A few steps from the fire you stood holding nothing but a smoking stick, a few red coals glowing in the dark. But still.

Huffing. Definite. Loud. Breaths taken in, snorted out.

I stood up.

Mule deer could sound something like that. An alarm. A timid challenge.

They didn't, really, sound anything like this.

I shouted, "Hello?"

A quick retreat. Not wind, not rushing water. A gallop. Something big. Branches knocked aside.

Maybe a bull elk?

Probably not.

But it had run away. There was that.

I looked around, sized things up. The fire threw out a wavery ring of light maybe fifteen feet in diameter, cut off upwind by the trees, downwind by my poncho's snag. Toward the river, the little band of willows, and away, the cliff, a few glimmers off bits of rock. Beyond that, in every direction, dark as a pocket.

Rain began, ever so slightly, to patter down. "Fabulous," I said.

I went to my pack, the farthest reach of the firelight, toward whatever had been there, and pulled out my rain jacket, Park Service Gore-Tex, green and whispery against itself. With the hood up, I'd be deaf as a stone.

I left the hood down.

I walked my perimeter of light, picking up what pieces of wood I could find, adding them to the fire. Whatever it had been, it was gone now. I sat back down, gave another look around, took a big, easing breath, let it out. I picked up my book, flipped through the pages till I found Doc and the boys. The bigger fire was great, easier to read by, though, with the rain picking up, I had to hunch forward to keep the drops from pocking the pages.

Instead of the huffing, what came next could only be described as a roar. A holy shit, straight to your feet, bowel clamping, MGM lion roar. Eyes wide, I stared into the wind, which kept anything out there from smelling how hugely dangerously human I was. I couldn't see an inch farther than I could with my tiny fire. The edges of the trees were only brighter, the darkness beyond them only blacker.

Another roar. Branches breaking. Something thrashing. Or being thrashed.

"Hey," I shouted. "*I'm* the top of the food chain!"

Like hell.

Silence. But no charging retreat.

"Goddamn it," I whispered.

And then a thought. Pancoast. If he'd managed to sneak up here during the day, camp out, wait for me . . . This was *exactly* the thing he'd do. Did bears really roar, anyway? Or was that cartoon stuff, Tarzan dramatics? He'd be standing just beyond the light, biting his fist, fighting not to pee himself.

"Pancoast?" I shouted. "I'm dying here. I mean, you got me. Hysterical."

Nothing.

I picked up my torch, held it up high and out front. I took a step toward my pack. Another.

The roar and the rattle of branches stopped me dead. I shouted, not quite quaver-free, "The highest form of humor, Pancoast. I mean it."

One more step, and I slipped my hand into the side pocket of my pack, pulled out my service revolver, a five-shot .38, a gun the boss had chosen, insisting the river rangers carry guns but wanting something that wouldn't get in our way, so going small, something that fit into the palm of my hand. We couldn't even shoot the same ammo the rest of the rangers used, for fear the gun would blow up. A cork-on-a-string kind of gun, when what was called for here was a bazooka. An air strike.

I pointed it into the night. In my other hand, I held a smoking stick. A few embers glowing red. Was a flashlight really so expensive?

I tossed my stick back to the fire, and searched what I could see of the tree trunks, looking for one I might possibly climb. No real likely candidates. But in a pinch? Grizzly canines clapping at my ass? Possible. Whatever was out there, though, would be on me before I lifted a foot off the ground.

I grabbed the lowest branch of the most realistic tree. Tugged.

Just beyond the light there was a sudden tussle, a tearing sound. Something being pulled out of the ground, rending and gnashing. A chokecherry pulled up by the roots? An eighty-foot spruce?

I lifted myself off the ground. But if I could get up, then what? When could I come down? Daylight? Spend the next ten, eleven hours perched on a branch I hoped could hold my weight? Ten hours in the dark, the rain, which was getting more serious about coming down.

I put my foot back on the ground. Pointed my little gun.

"All right, Pancoast," I shouted. "This is your best one ever. No lie. But I'm kind of over it. One more roar, and I'll shoot your ass."

The roaring stopped. The rending and tearing and stomping.

What the hell was out there?

"Come out into the light now. Bring your beer. I'll laugh myself sick."

Nothing but the breeze again. The creek. The rain.

I stepped backward to my fire, only glancing away from whatever might come out of those trees long enough to avoid stepping into the flames.

Footsteps, sounding closer. Huffing.

Not a roar, but I fired anyway. Up high, into the tree-tops.

Small as it was, the clap of that gunshot closed in between the cliff walls and clouds, the rip of the flame out the barrel end startled me so much I nearly missed the freight-train charge of full retreat through the trees. Not even Pancoast could make that one up. Nor could an elk.

I pulled up my hood. The rain drummed down against it. I edged it back, tucked it behind my ears. But there'd be nothing more to hear. Right? Thing was probably unconscious this very second, the spruce he'd crashed into cracked and listing.

How the hell do they get around in the black like this anyway?

I squatted by my fire. Threw in the last of my collected wood. Worked on getting my breathing right again. Listened to my heart drum.

He'd been trying to get by me. On his way down the creek. The cliffs limited the options. He could splash down the creek, but that would only get him another twenty, twenty-five feet away from me. Or, he could just run right over me. How much did fire bug them?

Or he could scare me senseless, make me run down that creek before him. Not a bad plan. If I had a headlamp, any kind of light, I'd be doing that right now.

But without the light I'd end up in the same cartoon I'd imagined him in, conked out beside whichever tree I hit first.

We had no options. Either one of us.

Which is what I told him, when he came back.

He didn't roar this time. Just padded up close, knocked around a few branches. As if he'd been upstream doing some option exploring of his own, maybe hoping I'd gone away as much as I'd hoped he had. I thought maybe just once I caught a trace of movement at the very last reach of the fire's light, which was waning, closing in, the wood all gone.

I ran my finger along the tiny gun's trigger. It really was a ridiculous thing. I didn't want to shoot again, figuring it might take all of the last four shots to put myself out of my misery as the bear dined on my haunches.

I stood again, not knowing if showing him my size was a good plan or bad. I stepped back to the fallen snag of my poncho, and untied my boots. "I'm going to bed," I yelled. The poncho would be an even better hood, the rain against it deafening me to whatever might be taking place beyond it. I could not listen to this all night.

"You can take the creek, or just run past me here," I said.

"Or you can stay the hell upstream for the rest of your

fucking life!" I shouted, firing once more into the treetops and struggling out of my rain jacket, dragging it under the poncho with me as I kicked into my sleeping bag, zipping it up tight, pushing my better right ear into the pillow of my wadded wool shirt, my not-so-hot left ear only inches from the steady thwapping of raindrops against the rubber sheet. The teddy bears could have their whole goddamn picnic right in my fire ring, and I'd be none the wiser.

Trying hard not to imagine the crack my femur would make, the sucking tear of muscle torn from bone, I curled into a ball, back against the dead tree's trunk, and closed my eyes. Long before the boys scrambled my sleep patterns, I was asleep before the bear came back.

If he came back. If he ever left.

It was barely gray dawn when I woke, the drizzle steady, the poncho still blocking off the world, sight and sound both. I stretched, unzipped. Paused. Waited. I hunched my shoulders, wriggling against the ground till my head cleared the poncho, the rain cold against my face. No bear leered down at me. I wriggled some more, sat up. Fog wreathed the trees, hung heavy above the water. I pulled my gun out of my boot, stuffed my feet into them instead. Everything dripped, all color stripped away. Nothing moving but water.

I moved as if stealth were required, edging a boot up on the tree trunk, tugging the laces tight. Keeping my eyes pointed upstream to the line of trees, I stuffed my bag, rolled the poncho around the pad, and tied everything into place on my pack, zipped up the pockets.

I lifted the pack, nothing on my mind since I'd cracked open my eyes but flight, hasty retreat, getting the hell out of

Dodge. But now, standing with my empty pack barely weighing down a shoulder, I knew I couldn't not look. I set my pack down.

Holding my gun out front, I stepped farther upstream than I had all day yesterday, into what had been the black. I only made it half a dozen steps when I came to an arc of torn-up ground, the limit of the bear's nerve. Small limbs lay scattered about, bitten off or torn down. Sap oozed from fresh rips in the trunks of the bigger trees. The earth itself had been gouged down to bare mud, a tangle of overlapping footprints, long claws. The few whole tracks looked more than a foot long. The arc extended all the way from cliff to creek, the bear looking for a slot to make his break.

In the tangle, I had no way to see if he'd made that break, if, this morning, he was still upstream, where every step I took toward Pancoast would leave him farther behind, or if he'd slipped by, and now I'd be walking up on him from behind.

I went back to my pack. Pulled it up, tightened the straps. Thirty feet downstream, my beach gave out and I stepped into the creek, gasping as the water crossed my boot tops. The rain murmured down. I stomped and splashed the miles, calling out to the bear, obscenities, jokes, whatever I could think of.

When I reached the last gasp of the Pilgrim Creek road, I saw the green Dodge parked at the end of a long pair of Pancoast skid ruts, the windows fogged inside. I woke Pancoast with a quick slap against the driver's door.

He rolled down his window, stretched. "How about this weather?" he said.

I dropped my pack in the back, circled around to the passenger side, pulled my rain jacket off, and threw it into the backseat, then dropped down in front, the rain tinny on the roof. I studied Pancoast long enough that he said, "What?"

"Where were you last night?"

"What? At home. Dry as a popcorn fart."

"Uh huh," I said. I eased back into the seat, let my shoulders relax for the first time since the evening before. "You know," I said, "I could have killed you."

He spun the truck around, back wheels chattering, gravel flying, and didn't ask.

21

Bob Marshall Wilderness, Montana
May 2004

Stepping out to the root cellar, I spook four elk. I whisper, "Sorry," and hunch my shoulders, trying to make myself smaller, but I spook more across the airstrip and into the trees. The robin shoots out of her nest when I come back to the cabin. Only going through the motions, I can't step outside without disturbing something.

Before the morning outhouse run, I check through the windows, make sure the coast is clear, that I can slip out without forcing something into retreat. Propping the door open for the best outhouse view in the world, I pick up my reading material, what I'd replaced the tattered 1989 issue of *Western Horseman* with: a collection of Roger Angell's baseball essays from the midseventies. My own baseball fever first took hold about that time, dashing out to do my paper route in Milwaukee, sifting through the sports pages to see if the Brewers had fallen yet again, a result depressingly easy to predict. Now I read that at one point the Brewers' *team* batting average had been .185. One eighty-five. They really had been that dismal.

My sophomore year, my father, about as far from a frivolous man as it is possible to imagine, stunned me by writing, unasked, a letter to the principal, explaining that I would be unable to attend school on the day of the Brewers' home opener. A rite of passage, he called it, a springtime ritual. Not a father-son ritual, apparently, but a ritual nonetheless. I was on the bus to the stadium, by myself, before I could quite believe he'd cut me loose.

In addition to this unbelievable letter, my sudden enthusiasm brought stories out of my parents. They'd been to County Stadium only two days before the birth of my sister Terry. Two weeks overdue, my mom recalled the sweltering temps, describing it in such detail that for years, even as I worked summers lifeguarding in the Nevada desert, it remained my picture of heat. My dad remembered that Warren Spahn had pitched a one-hitter against the Phillies.

I'd felt the grumblings of jealousy, wishing it had been my birth that had delayed itself long enough for a Spahn one-hitter, and, perhaps by way of atonement, my dad told me that two days after my twin and I were born, he'd accepted the rare offer of a ticket to the opener of the World Series, Braves versus Yankees. (My brother and I weighed in at eight pounds, one ounce and eight pounds, nine ounces. My mother opted not to attend.) Spahn won again, and my father waxed poetic about his pick-off move to first, at the same time saying Spahn was probably the homeliest man in

Milwaukee. One of his teammates said that if Spahn had a noseful of nickels he'd be a millionaire.

Through all of this I'd been stunned most by the revelation that my parents had discovered baseball before I'd been able to show it to them. That, maybe, they'd had lives before mine.

I close Angell's book, leaving Milwaukee and my early teens behind, returning to Gates Park, my midforties. The day, I notice at last, is once again overcast, the sky threateningly dark down Biggs way. The radio's weather report called for more like yesterday, but the sky doesn't agree. Jeans or shorts? Rain gear stuffed into the backpack or not?

In the end, I pull on jeans, pack my raincoat but not pants, then, shuttering the cabin, giving the sky a few sideward glances, I leave the raincoat hanging on a nail on the front porch, only later realizing it probably kept the robin frantic all day long.

Moving into the timber, I get the first few bars, or drumming bass lines or whatever, of Pearl Jam's "Who You Are" stuck in my head, and I hum it and whistle it, oompah it and slap it out against my chest as my bear warning, throwing in "Ode to Joy" and "Carmina Burana" now and then just to keep the bears off balance.

I look out across the river, where the calf, maybe a day old, had met its end, then thump and shout my way through the dark stuff and on to Spruce Creek, no bears leaping out from behind any trees.

Once on my way to Biggs, I plod along by rote, not much different than a horse, when a flicker darts past, only a foot in front of my face. I rear back and watch it bob into the burned aspen grove, disappearing among the tall, silvery trunks.

I follow after, hoping to find a nest hole, but only find myself lost in a forest of dead young trees, ten- and twelve-foot trunks, big around as the business end of a baseball bat. A thicket of walking sticks, I think, tugging on one, breaking it free of its decaying roots. I'd read that aspen propagate through runners, that an entire grove could be considered a single living thing, one of the largest organisms on the planet. I saw off the thin end, leaving myself a staff five and a half feet long, knurled at the top where the roots had branched off but silky smooth below, trenched here and there by old scars, the edges smoothed by new growth around old damage.

Back on the trail, I thump my stick against the rock, a solid *thwump*, a warning for bears, something to lean on, a perfect feel to the hand. I smile, thump it again.

I pull Aidan's notebook out of my shirt pocket and discover his name scrawled across the top of the first four pages, some partially erased, others scratched out, but they all look perfect to me. I flip far away, saving them, and make my notes, things to remember to tell him, as instructed.

Out on the flats, there isn't a trace of an elk. I stop, scanning up and down, out across the fall toward the creek, up toward the rise of the mountains. Nothing. "Where the hell is everybody?" I ask aloud, and a badger explodes out of the horse-trenched trail ten yards ahead of me, dashing up the hill and throwing itself into a hole. A crisp, neat, headfirst plunge.

Without realizing it, I'm crouched back, brandishing

my stick like Little John's staff, and I have to catch my breath before moving forward to inspect the hole. But it's just an empty black mouth, giving up no secrets.

I spook two whitetail bucks out from the eggs' spring, who, after their initial flush, walk back, watching me work at the buckets. Popping the first black lid, I discover eggs with tails *and heads!* They've managed to shuck the egg casings. The fry swim through the mesh of the observation basket, down to the dark safety of the biosaddles as soon as their world lights up. I glance to the deer, say, "You've got to see this!"

Back up top, I stop at the reading tree, knocking back an orange and another day in the life of Nick, more than a day even, the wardens after him, Nick and his sister on the lam.

I make the rest of the trek in good time, glancing at my watch as I cross the pack bridge, the boys' last day of school. It's an early out, 1:15 instead of 2:40. Only minutes left till they hit the door, I push hard, hoping to find some sweet fishing hole to cast into at the same time the boys finish their last day of school. Throwing what celebration I can.

Above the falls I veer to Gates Creek, working a half mile of twisting water without a strike, plowing upstream, shoving through the willows, the short and narrow casting lanes, frustrated with the stumbling, the punji point sticks of every beaver-nipped stem, the drop-to-your-waist canals of their pathways, just as likely to get steamrollered by a moose as mauled by a grizzly. Crossing the creek one more time, cursing away the bears instead of singing to them, I stumble right into an entire school of cutthroat, sending them into a panicked upstream scatter.

I cross the water, slip in the dirt cutbank, going all the way down. I lie there, huffing and puffing, my celebration something of a disaster. But, rolling onto my back, I see the cutthroat regather right where I'd crossed the stream. I check my watch, the bell ringing at Roosevelt. I pull the hook out of the cork butt and, still lying down, shoot a cast at them, all of ten feet away.

I sit for half an hour catching every one of those fish at least once. But they won't give up their spot, won't give up striking at the fly. The perfect place, the perfect fish, to teach the boys to fly-fish.

Yet on my own, it's a pale celebration, and I pack it in, standing stiffly to finish the last little slog into the cabin.

Whatever the robin might have thought, I'd been wise to leave my raincoat. The sky has cleared off, leaving nothing but the sun, the occasional shade of the big, harmless puffballs of drifting cumulus. A blazing seventy-two by the cabin-porch thermometer, every fly inside is awake and droning, sounding like the deck of an aircraft carrier at war.

I retreat to my hammock, but minutes later one of the innocent cumulus bulks into a thunderhead, and I make it to the cabin just before a pounding, driving rain cuts loose, big fat drops crashing down, the temp dropping fifteen degrees in a minute.

As Sage used to say, answering any tourist's weather bitching, "Springtime in the Rockies!" Once the two of us were sitting in the ranger station when a couple of middle-aged sports blew through the door, rigged out in their chest waders, vests sprouting every bell and whistle any stack of catalogs could offer. "Where they catching all the fish?" one of them bellowed. Without missing a beat, Sage hooked a finger inside his mouth and yanked at his cheek. "Right here."

I stand on the porch, grinning as the rain drives down. The boys would be tearing out there into it, laughing and splashing.

I cut out the rest of Nolan's moccasins, then, back in the hammock after the deluge, the sun shining down, the grass sparkling, I sew them together. Five elk lie in the middle of the runway, keeping an eye on me but not worried enough to stand up.

I stand and stretch, then head in to put water on for pasta, and while it works its way up to heat, I make a trip to the outhouse, another saga of ancient baseball. But as I pick up Angell's book, something catches my eye at the far edge of the airstrip. Something big and dark, moving toward me out of the trees and lumbering along the airstrip. Big and dark, with no discernible head or neck. My first thought is, What in the world is a cow doing clear up here? It's that big.

But, really, I know what up here is that big, and clasping my pants up, I dash for the cabin, the binos. I get the creature locked in for about five seconds before it plods back into the trees. A huge grizzly, Angus-size, just ambling along. His rump and shoulders are chocolatey-dark, his midsection lighter, like a silver-backed gorilla, and his face and head lighter still, blond.

I run out to the buck rail, scan the trees for a long time, but never catch another glimpse of him. "Great," I say. "Now I have to carry bear spray to the *outhouse*. Sing 'Take Me Out to the Ball Game' while otherwise engaged." Even so, I can't stop smiling, the sight of the bear moving along so easily. Perfectly right.

At the same time, I realize I no longer feel any need to use the outhouse, and I smile, thinking I'd never before had the shit scared *into* me.

By seven the elk have returned to the runway, some whitetails as well. A few coyotes talk back and forth, but mostly it's a quiet, still night. A big bug hatch fills the air, backlit by the setting sun, sparkling. The swallows cut through them, darting like fighters. Returning to the cabin, I start cutting laces for Nolan's moccasins.

Then, out of nowhere, the forest radio crackles out, "Gates Park, Choteau."

I freeze, the scrap of leather paused against the knife edge stuck in the piece of kindling. If the sky had spoken, it would have hardly been a bigger surprise.

"Gates Park, Choteau."

I nearly tip over my chair. Leap the two steps to the desk at the head of my bed, grab the mic. "Gates Park," I say, talking to someone other than myself.

"Hello Gates, we have a message for you from Rose. It's not an emergency, but Aidan . . ."

He doesn't take a breath between Aidan and the next word, not even a glimmer of a pause, but in the routine space between two words my whole world trembles. What can have happened that's not an emergency but is still worth the only radio call I've ever received here?

He goes on, without interruption, "but Aidan's baseball coach has died, and she thinks you'd want to send condolences."

"Okay," I say. "Thanks."

"That's all," he answers. "Sorry about the coach."

"Me too," I say. "Thanks for the message."

"You have a good night. Choteau clear."

I click the mic back into its place.

Aidan's coach, Jack. The grandfather who'd thrown me the knuckler, who'd helped his grandson warm up, who'd shyly helped out anywhere needed, which was pretty much everywhere.

A week before I came into Gates, Aidan's team had its best showing ever, batting around each of the first two innings, Coach Jack pitching to them, happy as a little kid himself, trotting to the dugout after the first inning, crowing, "Boys, that's starting to look like *baseball* out there!"

After their second bat around the order, Jack jogged off the mound, pounding his mitt with satisfaction, a grin on his face he couldn't shake off. As he crossed the third base line he did this odd, falling spin move, landing flat on his back. For an instant it looked like a seventy-eight-year-old's attempt at Ozzie Smith's famous flip, and for less than that instant, I thought, "Jesus, Jack, are you trying to kill yourself?" but I was already jumping toward him, my mind catching up. Heart attack.

No pulse. A few agonal breaths. Somebody came to his head, my finger still on his carotid. I said, "I'm not getting anything here."

The guy at his head said, "I'm going to give him a few breaths."

I looked up. It was Jack's son, Ron, a fireman, who hadn't been at the game a minute before. The father of another player, another fireman on Ron's crew, came and took the chest. We started CPR. I kept the airway open for Ron. A mother from the other team, a nurse, came and helped. Someone ushered the kids away. An ambulance arrived. They cut open Jack's shirt and windbreaker, and I saw the scars of old heart surgeries marring his still-fit chest. They hit him again and again with a portable shock kit, and his heart started beating on its own.

They wheeled him away, his son going in the ambulance with him.

A father on the team came up and asked, "What just happened here?"

I shrugged. "The end, probably."

Rose and Nolan arrived about the same time as the ambulance. She rounded up Aidan, and he asked, "Is Jack going to die?"

"He might," I said, starting to collect the baseball gear. "His heart is tired and it stopped working."

For a couple of days, Jack's recovery had been remarkable. I visited him in the hospital, and he was all smiles, showing the different pitch grips on the baseball he'd asked for. But a few days later, a series of strokes hit, making the end inevitable.

I turn off the radio, look across the quiet cabin, wondering how Rose thought I'd send condolences. Smoke signals? But I sit back down, push aside the leather strings, and start a note to Jack's widow. What does one say? I remember his excitement at that last game, his child-like glee. "This is starting to look like *baseball*!" Not, really, a bad way to go out.

Sage had a toast he'd use now and then, "Here's looking up your old address!" I never really understood it, but always liked the tongue-in-cheek sound of it. So, stowing the leather gear for another day, taking my last little stroll in the failing light, I call out, "Here's looking up your old address, Jack." And then, quietly, as I turn to go inside, I add, "Play ball."

But, though it's "Take Me Out to the Ball Game" I try to hum for him, it's Billy Bragg that overwhelms me. "Kiss me goodnight and say my prayers / Leave the light on at the top of the stairs / Tell me the names of the stars up in the sky / A tree taps on the window pane / That feeling smothers me again / Daddy is it true that we all have to die?"

Grand Teton National Park, Wyoming
Fall 1987

After six full seasons in the Tetons, I was thirty years old, and Sage, my mentor, sixty-five. Despite the river, my absolute love of pushing a boat out onto those waters, I chafed more and more against the protocols and paperwork of the Park Service, the idiocy of bureaucracy, the reams of rules and regulations, the yoke of my boss's neuroses. And Sage, ageless as he was, wondered about how much fun it still was, if it was worth the work of pulling up stakes every spring in Arizona, moving to Wyoming, then back again in the fall, the whole snowbird migration.

Edging around the idea of leaving paradise, joking about only leaving together, we made a compact: neither of us would leave until the other was ready, too. A "one, two, three, go!" kind of thing. Like kids. Partners in crime, neither he nor I could imagine being the one to leave the other behind.

But Sage still began every day driving from his home up Pacific Creek, down to my old homestead cabin. Coming in for the keys to his government truck, he'd find me sitting alone at the window-side table, reading or writing. Now and then, reaching past me, he'd lift the bottle of whiskey from the windowsill and unscrew the top, carefully pouring himself a tiny cap full. Tossing it back, he'd smack his lips, shake his head, and say, "Ah, a little mouthwash, don't you know."

Over the years, he'd seen how more and more often it was a notepad I hunched over rather than a novel, knew how if I worked a six A.M. shift, I'd be up at four, scribbling away. A certain sense of privacy kept him from ever asking to see a word of it, but he liked to talk about the whole mechanics of creativity, marveling over the idea of being able to shape other places, make real people come to life in your head. In the navy, he'd served on his cruiser, the *Brooklyn*, with a yet-to-be-known Lenny Bruce, and after the war he hung out at cafés with him, listening to him and Henny Youngman and Sid Caesar work their lines on each other. He said the same thing about Lenny's mind, how it just went places other people's never had. "That and he was just a crazy bastard," he said, going into stories about their New York City leaves together.

Then one day in the fall of that sixth year, he swished his mouthwash around, smacked his lips, shook his head, and waved down to my notebook. "Kid," he said. "I'd love working here with you till my last breath, but you can't stick around here for me. Or for anyone. You've got to give it a shot. You've got to get out of here, do what you love to do."

I said I kind of thought I was doing what I loved to do, but he laughed and said, "You'll always be playing. Nobody on earth is going to stop that. But, really, this place is for people who don't have anywhere else to go. And you," he pointed to my notebook, "well, you've just got to give yourself the chance."

Always be playing. I looked up at him. Once he'd held up a mile of traffic at an entrance station as he leaned into a station wagon, reading *One Fish, Two Fish, Red Fish, Blue Fish,* calming a squalling baby. Hell, he was the guy who taught me how to turn my patrol boat into a water bed, showed me that the park boundaries were more a theory than a fact.

Every spring we were required to take a week of law-enforcement refresher training, culminating with firearms qualification at the gun range, a backstop berm dozed up in the sagebrush. We had to shoot during the day and again at night, and as his night vision failed, he first asked me to throw a few extra shots into his target but then came up with the real solution, noticing that the U.S. government pens we all carried in our chest pockets were pretty darn close to the diameter of a .38 caliber slug. Coming up to check out his target while our boss, the range master, tallied scores down the line, he'd punch his pen through his human silhouette target again and again, then slip his pen back into his pocket and wait for his score. Only once did he get overenthusiastic, our boss squinting, aiming his flashlight more carefully, recounting, but still coming up with two bull's-eyes over the maximum possible. "Fromm," he said to me, "you must be getting a little wild; you're not even hitting the right target." I confessed to being a little shaky.

And when I'd broken my shoulder, he'd opened up my world just by putting me into the copilot seat of his truck as he set off on his mysterious rounds.

While it was true that he'd lived sixty-five years, that hardly gave an approximation of his age. Once, while I drove near the Oxbow Bend, on "patrol," a call came over the radio about skinny-dippers near Cattleman's Bridge. A Lodge Company tourist group had complained. Practically there already, I called back that I'd take care of it.

I turned down the dirt road, a hot, gorgeous, August day, thinking skinny-dipping sounded just about perfect, that I'd be tracking down geniuses. My radio crackled again. "465, 462." My call number, Sage's, all very protocol. I answered back with my own. "465."

"I'll take care of this one, Pete."

"Already there, Sage. Don't bother."

"I'm at Cattleman's myself," he said, sounding almost out of breath. "And those swimmers appear to have left the area."

I said, "Ten-four," and rolled on, the road a dead end half a mile ahead. We could meet, have lunch, a picnic back in this ignored little corner of the park. But before I found Sage's truck, I found Sage, coming out of the aspen by the river, his uniform darkened under the chest, the arms, inside the thighs of his green jeans. How you'd get, say, if you'd rushed soaking wet into dry clothes. Behind him came two waitresses from Signal Mountain Lodge, girls in their twenties, their shorts and tank tops in the same sort of condition as Sage's uniform.

Sage tried, for a second, to keep a straight face, but when

I stopped in the center of the road, stepped out of my truck, and said, "I'm afraid I'm going to have to take you all in," the three of them couldn't hold it in.

"I was just showing these lovely visitors an area of the park overlooked by most tourists."

The girls giggled, and I gave the three of them the quarter-mile ride down to the collapsing bridge, to their Volkswagen, Sage's truck. We watched them drive off, and Sage said he'd just met them at the bridge, accidentally, that they got talking about skinny-dipping. "But they didn't think they could do it," he said, amazed. "So I walked them upstream, to that one little spot. You know it."

I did know it.

"I told them they could do anything."

I nodded. I knew that talk, too.

Sage, coming in for his capful of mouthwash every morning, saw me rising up out of my imaginary world more and more reluctantly. He knew I'd started to send stories out to magazines, had started to think more seriously about getting serious about it. But, still, it was leaving paradise. It was leaving Sage.

Then that fall, Pancoast and I ravaging the local goose population, we decided to put on a Thanksgiving-day feed. Snow poured down, and after work I slipped and slid my little pickup all the way up to Great Falls, chained up through the whole Gallatin Canyon, every iced twist and turn, burrowing down the flurry-rushed tunnel of my headlights. I spent the night in Great Falls and turned right back around first thing the next morning with Rose, the usual six-hour trip taking nine.

We had our feed, our winter wonderland party, Sage donning his ceremonial celebration necklace, a series of strung-together elk turds, fish vertebrae, and the cannon bone of some tiny calf. The woodstove stocked full to bursting, goose carcasses littering the table, the night black as coal, etching frost across every window, we drank toast after toast. Rose had to be back to work on Monday, but that was my last day—a turn-in-the-badge-and-gun, sign-some-paperwork waste of a day, one that, traditionally, people skipped out on, having the more local guys hand in their stuff for them. Pancoast had my back.

But the boss showed up on Saturday while I was packing my truck and said I couldn't skip work, that it was a duty day, that if I left, he'd take action. I can't remember what all he said, but I still feel the burn over how I gave in, how I drove Rose home on Saturday, drove all the way back down on Sunday, and, power trip complete, the boss let me sign the paperwork, took my gun and badge himself, and, all pals, told me he'd take care of it, that I should take the rest of the day off, hit the road early.

Sage, stopping by to say good-bye on his way to Arizona, only gave me a look, said, "You've got to get out of here."

So, finally, with Sage's blessing, at Sage's urging, I left the mountains and rivers behind, off to make my life as a writer.

But only a few months later in Montana, my friend Guy, a pro football player, hearing of this, had a contractor he was hiring to renovate a house in Missoula call me up, explain that Guy would not give him the job unless he hired me. I told him I didn't know what he was talking about, that

I had zero experience as a carpenter. "Well, you'll get it, but I don't get this job unless you come to work."

I called Guy, who told me, "I just figured, if you're going to write for a living, it might, you know, kind of be a good idea to learn a trade."

So I worked for two years, learned a trade, built up my first-ever nest egg, then quit again, two years of income in the bank, two years free to start earning my keep with words.

One book came out. Another. Another. Rose and I, kids something we decided we were ready for, married, she however reluctantly, a run down to Jackson, the courthouse lawn, Pancoast and his wife our witnesses. It would be easier for the kids, I figured, and from then on, what else mattered?

Nolan was born. Aidan. More books. School. And through it all, at every next step into the unknown, every impossible thing, Sage's maxim, "Kid, you can do anything."

On Sage's mantel there was a picture of him, in his full class A dress uniform, shaking hands with Jimmy Carter beside a helicopter near Jackson Lake. He'd been part of the cordon line of rangers protecting the landing sight, instructed by the Secret Service to keep their backs to the helicopter, to let the photos be taken, to keep anyone from getting close to the president. Instead, as soon as Carter touched a foot to the ground, Sage wheeled and marched straight to him, stuck out his hand, and said, "President Carter, Sagebrush DeGroot, best goddamned ranger in the National Park Service. I'd like to personally welcome you to Grand Teton National Park, my jewel in the Park Service's crown." Carter looked a little startled. The photographers snapped away.

At sixty-five, he still looked forty, wrestled with me constantly, so when, years after we'd both retired from the Tetons, I saw him back in the park with an oxygen tank, a hose running up to his nose, I could not have been more surprised. Pulmonary fibrosis. Idiopathic, he told me, no known cause, no known cure. He explained he was at thirty-percent oxygen. Up from twenty. "When I get to a hundred, and then need more . . ." He tilted his head to the side, a kind of shrug. "Well, then, lights out for SOB." SOB: Sweet Old Bob.

Twelve years after he urged me out of the park, insisted I write, I was working on my eighth book, set in West Texas. He'd settled permanently in Santa Fe by then, and when I had to go to Pecos for research, I called, said I might as well fly to Albuquerque, drive over to visit, then head down to Pecos. He said that would be great, and I bought the plane ticket. A few days later, his wife, Blackie, called, told me what Bob would never tell me, that he wasn't doing at all well. She wanted to know how soon I could come. I moved my flight up, and the day before I left she called again, said, "You better come right now."

He'd started to suffocate the night before, needing more than one hundred percent, and, despite the hospice, the DNRs, he, the world-record-holding swimmer, had felt himself drowning and panicked, asked Blackie to call the ambulance. He was in the hospital now, on a respirator. I was there in the afternoon. He couldn't talk, but he could still smile, something it seemed he was never far from.

I sat with him and told stories, then sat with the family and talked over what to do. We all knew, though. Sagebrush, here? Sweet Old Bob? It was the last thing he wanted. He just couldn't go out drowning. I knew what that was about. Had seen it over and over. Had imagined it for myself again and again.

The following summer, they held a memorial service for him in the Tetons. I spent the afternoon fishing in some of the old haunts, then walked out to our ball field (known ever since my eventful play at first as Fromm Memorial Stadium) to await a ride to the festivities. It was quiet there, the weeds and grass making inroads on the base paths, the sagebrush retaking the outfield. They didn't, it seemed, play much ball down here anymore.

Winding my way out to my spot in center, dodging the gopher holes, the glacial rock, and sage, I stumbled across a lost baseball mitt, Eric somebody inked across the leather, a faded name I didn't recognize. It was June, the mitt obviously there over at least a couple of winters. I slid my fingers into the soggy leather, opened and closed the glove. Once Sage had told me of a German air attack on his cruiser, off the coast of Italy. "I stood there staring up at those tiny planes like it was some kind of air show, when an officer came up behind me, yanked my helmet from under my arm, and slammed it down on my head. He pointed up at the planes. 'DeGroot,' he said to me, 'you see those planes? Every single person up there, every goddamned one of them, is trying to kill *you*! Do you understand that?' " Even forty years later, his awe was still plain, that anyone had wanted to kill him.

I faced home, put my hands on my knees, the outfielder's ready position, and pictured him there on the mound, his theatrical windup building to the soft, underhand lob. I was waiting for my ride to his memorial service, and the snipe winnowed all around me.

I whispered, "Rootie-toot-tootie, another beauty for DeGrootie," one of his old lines, expressing excitement over anything. Everything. Something he was always doing. He'd never caught that whole "been there, done that" disease. Still a kid at sixty, seventy.

An old, old local settler, Stippy Wolff, still lived inside the park when we worked there, and Sage liked to visit him, pointing out how Stippy would stop and stare at the mountains now and then, the mountains he'd lived beside his entire life. He'd lose track of the conversation, of time, then slowly reel himself back in, smile, shake his head. "Don't the mountains look nice today?" he'd say, a line and attitude Sage never ceased to admire.

At home, Eric somebody's mitt is probably still on the floor just inside the front door, ready for a quick game of catch before dinner. A box of Sage's ashes rests on my desk in the basement, where I write, every day, just like he'd told me to.

Bob Marshall Wilderness, Montana
May 2004

The buzz of a mosquito wakes me, and I lie still in the dark, waiting for a pause to the whining hum, the feather touch against skin. I pounce, squashing it flat, and shoot both arms over my head in victory. Victorious, but hopelessly awake. Not quite five. A heavy mist lies over Gates, gray banks of fog oozing into the trees from the little pond at the end of the airstrip. The elk I spook vanish into it like wraiths.

Reminded by last night's call, I keep trying to check in with Choteau, something I've consistently forgotten to do, but can't raise a response. I cut lace holes in Nolan's moccasins, thread the laces through, try Choteau again. Still nothing. It isn't until I'm a mile down the trail that I realize it's Saturday, that no one is sitting by the radio in Choteau.

The warm weather has brought the river up half a foot,

the water completely opaque. I thump over the bridge, and charge up the hill, launch my pitch into the pond.

The day is completely different than yesterday's plod. I start in shorts, the wool singlet I'd won off a good-natured Maori guy in a pool game in New Zealand nearly a quarter of a century ago, though I still have trouble getting my head around anything in my life having happened a quarter of a century ago. The miles fall away without effort, nothing quite like a monstrous grizzly plodding by your outhouse for invigoration.

Reaching the northernmost edge of Biggs Flat, I find my eighty elk in the burned aspen, their favorite haunt. I sit, as before, and wait for them to stream past, but this time they bunch up and string out up the mountain, the pounding of their hooves echoing in my chest, a more than usually determined charge away from me. Skittish.

A few minutes farther on, way up the hill in the shade of a pair of unburned trees, I spot a lone cow that somehow, stance or something, looks odd, her back legs stretched behind her, her tail held high. She isn't grazing but has her head lowered, occasionally glancing back toward her rear. Sure I'm about to witness a calf's birth, I lie down beside the trail, rest my head in my hands, my elbows in the dirt, a firm rest for the binos, a little too close, perhaps, to the badger hole I'd discovered earlier. I'm in no rush to have him Tasmanian devil my ankle while I gaze up the hill.

Another cow wanders across the hillside, pausing beneath the trees, giving a sniff at the rear of the calving cow. The second cow saunters on, grazing as she goes. The calver turns around, lifts a hind leg, and reaches under herself, licking or nudging her lower belly. She seems to strain and stretch. Fifteen minutes pass, and then, without any progress, she moves off slowly, following the second cow, walking like she's not a bit comfortable. Together they wander over the side of the hill, out of sight.

On the edge of the drop to the creek, just beyond the reading tree, another thirty or forty elk lie bedded down at the edge of the timber, favoring the live green trees over the patches of blackened sticks. Another forty elk on the windward side of the trail bolt away, clattering through the burn toward the bear cub tree, a beautifully built six-point bringing up the rear. It's hard to believe how much bigger than the cows he is. They string into a single-file line, tawny against the blackened wood and low green weeds, pausing to stare back at me. The bull nips a few mouthfuls as he moves, but the lead cow is antsy, taking the herd over the top of the hill, out of sight.

Down at the buckets, about half the observation-basket eggs appear to be hatched, or hatching. Supposedly, hopefully, the same thing is going on with the huddled masses below the biosaddles. I perform my duties, snug the lids down tight, and scramble back up the hill to the reading tree.

The elk that had been bedded down in the timber to the east have moved close to the tree, and we stumble into each other. They spook up the hill, but not without complaint. The cows bark and yelp as they go, a little bull throwing in a halfhearted bugle. The big bull group that I'd spooked over the hill has filtered back into the burn, and he bugles in answer, nothing halfhearted about his eerie, grunting whistle.

The two groups really get going, back and forth, filling the air with their grunting and yelping, barking and bugling. Caught between them, it sounds like a day out of the Jurassic, like pterodactyls will be swooping down any minute. All I need is the crazy prehistoric whooping of a sandhill crane.

Finally it quiets down, or almost so. One elk keeps it up, an odd gasping bark every minute or two. Sounds like it's always from the same place, and I wonder if, instead of the bull, it's a cow, maybe in labor. The disadvantage of making such a noise in such a condition seems obvious, however, and, though I scope with the binos, I never find the noisemaker.

I push up and head to Spruce Creek, where, again, the eggs look to be hatching well. In the relative peace and quiet there, the rush and tumble of the creek and river providing white noise, I read "The Killers" before making the last push back up to Gates.

An overcast had been creeping in since I'd listened to the elk, some cumulus sidling in beneath the overcast, and now a dramatic south wind begins whipping across the park. The temperature drops fifteen degrees. Twenty.

A towering thunderhead boils in from the west, miles wide, black as night. I bring a chair onto the porch, with apologies to the robin, who flutters off to a pine to wait me out.

The thunderhead, however, though still building taller, rolls quietly past, off to terrorize the plains. But there are more behind it, complete with thunder and lightning, the rolling low rumbles growing sharper, more claps than booms. Wind flaps my shirt, my pant legs, ruffling through my heavy, dirty hair.

I can't help but smile, the extravagantly unleashed display, but then remember Tom's story of a guy getting hit by lightning one night here, his arm draped over the metal rail of the bunk bed. "That sat him up," he said. "Arm tingled for three straight days." I drop my chair legs down to the porch and move away from the big steel boxes of the radio's solar batteries.

By six o'clock I have to light a lantern to see enough to sew bags for all the treasures I've collected for the boys. Besides the bear turds, I have hair too, pulled from trees, from the plank railings on the side of the bridge, chips from a beaver-chewed tree, a couple of sticks meticulously pared of all bark, a pair of tiny cannon bones from a downed calf. I think maybe I'll dress up the pouches with gopher tails dangling from the drawstrings, feathers maybe.

The temperature down to fifty, I start a fire to cook on. By six thirty, the cabin's in a gap between squalls, sun pouring through the rain, lighting the next storm brewing over the mountains. Knowing exactly what the boys would do, I walk outside, soaking up the rain and sun both. A real monkey's wedding. When the next storm plows in, I go inside and stand dripping beside the stove.

Rain drumming on the roof, I sit at the table and watch it come down. Only nine o'clock, I shut down the lantern, crawl under the sleeping bag, and, taking a last look out the window, see a dozen wet elk grazing at the edge of the porch.

The next day, in the Hansel and Gretel stretch, I walk into the half-eaten elk calf, come cowering back to my cabin, everything tweaked just a bit off center.

24

Bob Marshall Wilderness, Montana
May 2004

I leave the Spruce Creek eggs on their own the next day, and the following morning the rattling of the cabin windows wakes me, squall after squall ripping through. Now and then thunder rumbles overhead, but mostly just these hard-charging storms, pelting rain, furious gusts. I make my break in a lull, stop at the far end of the pack bridge, glance up toward Spruce Creek, guess the half-eaten calf has long since been fully eaten, but still turn away for Biggs, give the bears a few more hours to digest, nap, pick their teeth, leave, whatever it is they do.

Clinging to hope, I wear shorts, figuring they'll be as warm as wet pants and my legs will dry more quickly without the soaking denim. The wind, though, as I break into the open burn, makes me wonder. My dad would call this a bitter day. But, truth is, I love weather like this. My Germanic ancestry showing through, all Wagnerian.

Staying ahead of a squall bearing down from behind, I jog a half mile across the flats, then slow to allow another to rush past in front. I can't help grinning, playing catch-me-if-you-can with the storms. I pull out a carrot, munching as I laugh, call out "What's up, Doc!" to the gray wall of rain sweeping Biggs. I swallow wrong, and suddenly I'm staggering along, gasping and sputtering, wondering how in the world I'll Heimlich myself out here in the middle of all this grass—run back to the burn? throw myself over a stump? I'll never make it. But I manage to swallow again, stand whooping in breaths, eyes watery with tears, with laughter. Surrounded by bears, wolves, I'll meet my end by the deadly carrot.

The flats' bluebirds are even more brilliant in the gloomy light, almost aglow as they flit against the black clouds. The word "cerulean" comes to me, probably off a tube of oil paint from high school art classes. It seems perfect, though without a dictionary, I'm not quite positive it even means "blue." Just pretty sure. One of those words you aren't normally able to toss into the course of a Montana conversation. My father's vocabulary bulges with words not ordinarily bandied about. Recently he'd told me it was a shame the word "scoundrel" had fallen into disuse. "With the current administration, it's certainly a word we should hear more of."

Passing the reading tree, the trail descending slightly toward the big drop into the creek, I cross through another little stand of aspen, this one not quite completely burned, and I realize how it has surprised me every day with its wonderful smell. It's just big enough for a couple of whiffs—then I'm through—but I realize I've smiled almost every day there, as I do again today, the earthy fall scent accentuated by the rain and wind.

Racing the storms, I reach the buckets in a little over an hour. The way the wind's swirled, it seems it's always been in my face, but in my game of dodging I've remained un-scathed, my life charmed.

I do my almost daily cleaning of the silty buckets, though the eggs in the observation basket continue to hatch. There are, on the other hand, several clumps of dead eggs, globby clusters that, though not growing the telltale fuzz of fungus, appear to be sticky, some hatchlings caught on them, wrig-gling to no avail. I do what I can to free them, poking a twig into the dead mass, breaking them apart, washing the dead pieces out through the exit pipe. Some of the hatch-lings swim free, but others seem doomed, no way to scrape them free without tearing them apart.

Starting back, dancing across the log over the creek, I work on counting. Twenty days now since I said good-bye to the boys. Triple any previous separations. While time has tempered the desolation of the first few days, it haunts me too, this stretch of days I'll never get back, the frenetic pace of their changes.

I pause at the pack bridge, the trip-trap path back home, then take a breath and pass it by, start up the hill toward Spruce Creek. I slow, studying the hillside of the first calf kill, pound my staff a little harder, as if expecting to see griz-zlies every time I pass.

Another squall skirts close as I approach the Hansel and Gretel stretch, hulking gloomier and spookier than ever, closed in under the black clouds, the wind deafening, the trees blinding. I shout and bang, take another breath, start Billy Bragg full volume. I don't have my bear spray out, my hand on the gun, but I have the zippers open on both sides of my raincoat, leaving everything accessible, and I step into the trees, searching as far as I can into the branches, the needles, the trail. I round the corner, shout, "Make a hole!" and the calf's spot is empty. Nothing at all. I shake my head, blink. I did not make this up, imagine it.

I bend lower, studying, and there, finally, is a hair, and then another, the crinkly white, hollow hair of elk. I follow them maybe ten yards off the trail, back into the thick trees. "Daddy is it true . . . ?"

And there lies what's left of it. Hair. Nothing else. Not a bone, not a hoof, not even the standard pile of greenish-brown mulch I've learned to expect at every kill site, the half-digested contents of the stomach, something no predator or scavenger has any interest in.

The calf, I realize, had never tasted grass. If it had lived long enough to eat anything at all, it had only been a few tastes of its mother's milk.

The dripping woods as dark and close as ever, I wallop my stick against a tree trunk, send a shower down from the needles, and shout, "Just checking my fish!" I start forward, back onto the narrow trail. "You guys know me by now! Just doing my job!"

I have an idea that they do indeed know me, that they've spent the last weeks watching me move up and down this trail. Have moved off and away long enough to let me pass, have followed behind when they had to, have even moved away from a kill without making a peep. They're used to me maybe. Tolerant.

Or, maybe, I'm just another item on the Chinese restaurant's lazy Susan, going round and round, the bears one day deciding, *Oh, okay, I'll try* that *one.*

Either way, I make it out the other side and slide down the Spruce Creek hill, grabbing everything I can to keep it from becoming a tumble.

The grayling, ignored for two days, seem no worse for it. A few swim up near the top of the saddles, but mostly they seem content staying down in what cover they have. Really, they're only doing what they do, and I wonder how much my daily checks have mattered.

My luck with the storms finally runs out while I huddle over the Spruce Creek buckets. The wind goes berserk, forty miles an hour, fifty, lashing the willows and pines, branches flailing and whipping, rain driving down horizontally. A burned tree crashes down across the river, cracking and booming, then another. Another. I yell, "Timber!" and the rain turns to hail and then snow. I hunker underneath a tight trio of pines. Over the howling gusts, I can't even hear myself laughing.

Then it's over, the sun showing through behind the squall, everything soft in the glistening light. I stand, jaw agape, taking in the blue humps of already-melting hail, the steam curling into the sunlight. Slowly, I go back to my buckets, find about two thirds of the eggs hatched and about half of those out of the observation baskets, either having left the exit spout or, more likely, joining their brethren beneath the biosaddles.

I linger over the eggs for more time than makes any sense, hoping the sun can open up long enough to make the dark stretch a little less menacing.

But I can't climb into the bucket, pull the lid shut over me, and finally I stand, seal the lids, and pull my way back up the hill, step back onto the main trail, face the return through Hansel and Gretel.

I only pause a moment before charging into those trees, shouting, "Kiss me goodnight and say my prayers / Leave the light on at the top of the stairs," as the pines brush against me.

Out the other side, I shout, "Made it!" and start laughing, running, racing another squall back to the cabin, beating it by seconds, dropping the shutters as the first fat drops strike, the wind flattening my jacket against me. Forty-three degrees, according to the porch thermometer.

I build up the fire. Sit and breathe. Grin.

For the rest of the afternoon, there's an unusual absence of game around, no deer or elk on the airstrip, none grazing into the willows beside the creek. Maybe, smarter than me, they're taking shelter in the timber. Or maybe my grizzly's lurking, a prankster, waiting to tip the outhouse as soon as I step inside.

But the wind drops to nothing in the evening, sunshine filling the park, sparkling on every dripping blade of grass, every pine needle. I go to the far side of the bunkhouse and buck up some firewood with a gigantic old bow saw I find among the firefighting gear. I fall into a rhythm, rocking back and forth, stove-length sections piling beneath the bucking rail. I kick them to the splitting stump and whack them into quarters, then eighths for kindling, starting to replace the wood I've been packing into the stove.

Consumed first by the rasping back and forth of the saw, the steady arcing shower of clean chips, and then by the rise and fall of the ax, the cracking, ripping tear of splitting wood, I don't notice the next storm building. But the wind gives it away, and I turn to a black wall reaching north and south, horizon to horizon.

I get my saw put away and gather up an armload of wood. The wind moans through the buck rails, the metal scaffold of the old weather station. A chorus of wolves would take me straight to Transylvania.

Coming back out for a second load, the drops strike like BBs. I pluck up the split wood, leaving the logs to the rain. Overloaded, a few sticks dropping down beside me, I lurch to the cabin, have to lean back into the door to close it against the gusts.

I drop the kindling into the wood box, brush the splinters from my shirt, the hail pounding like roofing hammers above me. I step out to the porch to watch the icy balls strike the ground, bounce back up a foot or so. The robin, for the first time, holds her ground, jumpy, eyeballing me from her perch. The thermometer reads thirty-six. Then thirty-four. Thirty-three.

I stoke the stove and stand before it, steaming.

25

Bob Marshall Wilderness, Montana
May 2004

The cabin gloomy around me, I take the first scalding sip of still-perking coffee and get as far as the date in my journal: *June 6th*. I set my cup down. D-day. Sixty years ago today. Rose's dad had landed on D+3. Confined to his bed at the end, cancer consuming him, he went back there for the first time, telling me stories no one had heard, stories of training in Ireland, goofing off, "borrowing" a train engine for a joy ride, then turning serious, of being overrun in the Bulge, just starting his first rest after five months of combat, how mad they'd been when they'd heard the predawn rumble of tanks, never guessing that they could be anybody's but their own, then running scared, dodging behind the German advance for days. At one point they ran into a river blocking their path, chunks of ice clogging the black water. Their lieutenant, a man he described only as "an asshole," couldn't swim. "We just left him there," he said. "Never heard from him again." Forty years later, confined to his bed, his own end in sight, he shook his head. "Being an asshole isn't something you should have to die for."

He never did say how or where he won the Bronze Star, never mentioned that it existed. He'd been dead now sixteen years. His medal sits on my desk, next to Sage's ashes.

It makes a near brush with an unseen bear seem like pretty small stuff.

Sitting alone in this cabin in the middle of the mountains, I wonder what, at my end, will seem anywhere near that big to me. I can't come up with any specific events. Only the boys, I hope. What a peaceful way to ease out, reeling through their lives, instead of fretting over somebody last seen half a century ago, beside an icy river in Belgium.

Thunder rolls down from the mountains, more rain, and I stand to scrub out my oatmeal bowl when the radio squawks, making me jump, but it's Tom calling to ask about the fish progress. I tell him about the hatching, that I plan to take the lids off the buckets today. Dave's with him, somewhere inside the Choteau ranger station, a place I've never been and can't picture. They tell me they've decided to ride in to Cabin Creek on Sunday, spend the night there, then meet me at Biggs Creek between twelve and one on Monday. We'll take apart the incubators, then ride up and dismantle the Spruce Creek site, then spend the night at Gates and ride all the way out on Tuesday.

I stand hunched over the desk, holding the radio transmitter in my hand. Out on Tuesday. I check the calendar on the desk. It's Tuesday now. Only a week left. Cutting me short two days.

I key the mic. "I don't know if the fish will have left the buckets by then," I say. "Far as I know, none have yet." The instructions Lee had left were explicit—leave the incubators operational until all the fry have left on their own.

Dave guesses that in six days, with the incubators opened, they'll be long gone. I say, "All right," and we sign off. I snap the mic back onto its hook. Two days early. Only a week left.

Suddenly, a week seems short. Even with the boys at the other end. But with the weather as bleak as it's been, maybe I'll be ready. Somehow, though, I doubt it.

Starting out for Biggs in full rain gear, the porch thermometer stuck at thirty-six, I tell myself again that I'll be getting back to the boys and Rose. I shake drops off my hood. The two days still feel like a loss. I won't be walking into any grizzly kills in Great Falls. No wolf calls or elk herds, osprey-chasing geese. The wildflowers replaced with daffodils, tulips. Bluebirds with sparrows.

The rain spatters down, a series of drizzles, the rain gear more useful as a block to the wind and the temps. The whitetail above the cabin put on a show, doing their nervous high-stepping prance before blowing out, bounding away, now and then throwing in huge, random leaps over nothing, as if they've been surprised by hidden springboards. Then, like a heron on a river always flying downstream, they settle down and wait for me to come plodding along, repeating the whole dash.

Once downstream of the pack bridge, the burns, out into the grassy flats, I walk beside the muddy gash of the horse trail as much as I can, vainly trying not to step on the ubiquitous wildflowers. Lupine had been strong last week, but the camas are overtaking them now. In between, shooting stars send up their delicate stalks, dandelions fill the gaps. There are more and more I don't know, one a miniature bear-grass-looking thing just beginning to get its head above the grass.

At Biggs, I lift the empty observation baskets out of the buckets, officially declaring the eggs hatched. Rain dribbles off my hood, ringing the surface, making it hard to see, but what fry I do spot swim frantically *down,* searching out hiding spots, nobody ready to make a break for the wide, wild world. They'll have to decide on their own. They have till Monday at noon. One week.

After cleaning out some of the sinisterly sticky egg clumps, I stack the bucket lids back in the trees, weighting them against the wind with rocks. I gather chunks of old rotting wood, balance them across the tops of the buckets, providing partial shade should the sun ever reappear.

Then, in case any of them decide to bust a move early, I dredge the creek from the incubators all the way down to Biggs Creek, spending far more time than necessary, creating a channel full-grown grayling could migrate through. Salmon. Belugas. It's work tailor-made for the boys— mucking around in sludge, ripping out branches, clawing out rocks, handfuls and handfuls of mud. Not much different than playing in the gutters at home, or Nolan clearing a path through the ice for the melt water to reach the sewer at the corner, a job he'd dedicate himself to through soaking boots, frozen hands, calls for dinner. I'd done the same kind of work as a kid and, admittedly, much older. In the

Tetons, Pancoast and I were ordered to test a portable fire-fighting water pump. Tossing its intake into the Snake and finding that it did indeed work, launching an impressive amount of water with impressive force, we killed the rest of the day fine-tuning hydraulic mining techniques—an eco-logical disaster in Smokey the Bear hats.

As seasonals, the low men on the pole, and river rangers at that, a kind of anchorless job, we were available for almost any task the permanents didn't care for. Like bound-ary marking. Or, one December, the only two seasonals left in the park, we were dispatched to the top of Signal Moun-tain to search for a small plane that had disappeared from radar shortly after taking off from Jackson Hole Airport. Strapping on snowshoes, we struggled for hours through thigh-deep powder, ambling around the airport side of the mountain, looking for a white plane buried in white snow, while the permanents chattered diligently on the ra-dio, searching from their cars and trucks, heaters on high. Clawing our way around a cliff face, pulling on whatever brush stuck above the snow, we listened to their elabo-rately useless procedures unfold over the crackling radio waves, and Pancoast suddenly jerked his radio off his belt holster, raised it to his mouth, and panted out our call let-ters, "700, 465." Just his out-of-breath voice drew every ear to its radio.

"700," the dispatcher answered calmly.

Pancoast shouted and panted into his radio. "Is this plane's . . . tail number . . . N72 . . . 41 . . . 39?"

Flustered, 700 said she'd have to check. There was com-plete radio silence during the minute she was away, an entire park poised and listening. Then she came back. "465, 700. That's negative."

The very voice of professional calm, Pancoast answered, "10-4. Disregard."

We fell howling into the snow, waiting, but no one had the courage to ask a single thing.

I chuckle halfway back across the flats.

I de-lid the Spruce Creek buckets, but they sit within yards of the river itself, no channels to muck out. Nothing to do but look in at the few swimmers, wish them luck, head home.

But the walk's a tough one, my waterlogged feet sore, and I'm glad to see the cabin. I collapse into the chair, look over at the woodstove, know I'll have to start another fire.

Eventually I sit forward, unlace my boots, kneel before the stove, stacking in the kindling, firing a match. I finish the boys' vests, the tail ends' tattered flanks and legs, holed and wild. They'll be thrilled by the idea of them, though I'm less sure they'll get much actual wear. A leather vest, the barbarian model, might not be the most practical wearing garment. Maybe a few camping trips. Halloween costumes.

I roll them up, stash them alongside their T-shirts. Only a week.

The rain gives up after dinner, and I take the chance to play with the cutthroats, working the creek all the way up to the enormous beaver dam, but again stopping there, turning back to the cabin, saving the water above for what I don't know.

I set the stove for the night, tired, hemmed in by rain. Being a short-timer doesn't help. I wonder if it wouldn't have been better to simply get it over with, dump the buckets and run, scram before the summer tourist season kicks in—other people back here something I just couldn't take. But I don't want out. I want in. And I don't want anyone else in here with me. Except the boys.

But the long walks. The bears.

Doesn't matter. As ever, I want it all.

26

Big Bend National Park, Texas
1985

One autumn in the Tetons a call came from Big Bend National Park in Texas, wondering if we might have a river ranger interested in working a winter season down on the Rio Grande. We did, and in January I drove from Montana to Wisconsin to see my folks, then down the Mississippi to New Orleans, then across the Gulf Coast to Baytown, Texas, to see my sister, and from there into the unknown of Big Bend, one of the few national parks that really is on the road to nowhere, a hundred miles back north to a grocery store, 125 to hit an interstate, the east-west I-10 at Fort Stockton.

Back in real desert for the first time since Lake Mead, I found the rescues here even more benign than those in the Tetons. There were none. In three months of floating the canyons, I met three other boats on the river, all in one day, during spring break. The rest of the time I floated solo:

two- and three-day trips through gorgeous canyons, ochre rock walls rising a thousand feet vertically from the water's edge. Or, my favorite, the seven-day trip through the wild and scenic stretch downstream of the park itself.

Silence was huge in the canyons, each creak of an oar-lock magnified and bounced back. Campsites, the skies scalded with stars, the light from the fire pushing up against utter darkness, felt as if they opened up on the entire rest of the world.

But it was on the water itself, odd as it may sound, that I learned to appreciate the desert again. For long stretches the river barely moved, slough-like flats of almost zero drop, the river hemmed in by cane, or rock, the hills beyond covered in mesquite and creosote. Then the canyon walls loomed, the river tightening, picking up speed, coming to life. Inside the canyon, rock broken from the sheer walls had nowhere to go but into the gorge, the river nowhere to go but over or around it. Rapids roared against the walls, announcing themselves in a gut-tightening way long before they were reached.

The solitude was almost otherworldly. No radio contact in the canyons or for the entire wild and scenic stretch. When the desert sun became too baking, the raft tubes growing too hot to touch, I splashed water across them. In quiet stretches, I edged into the water myself, drifting beside the raft, thought an awful lot of Mark Twain's stories of discovering the Mississippi from the pilot's house of a steamboat. Huck's simple line, "It's lovely to live on a raft."

My parents, though hardly raised on it themselves, started us camping: car affairs, state parks mostly, a tent, a picnic table, the fire grate, neighbors, carrying the five-gallon jerry can back from the pump, the weight of it tipping us sideways. And, though never a fisherman himself, my dad supplied us with spinning rods, the tangles of line, the chaos of tackle boxes. Of the six of us, I was the only one caught up by it, but as we got older, he did his research, heard Old Town was a respected name in canoes, and found a fiberglass behemoth. More research took us just across the state line to the Upper Peninsula's Sylvania Recreation Area, where we started a more basic type of camping, carrying only what we could fit into the canoe, lug across the portages. It was the wildest thing I had ever done, and I longed for it every summer, to sit in the rain, be feasted upon by the mosquitoes, to wake before anyone else and paddle out alone into the dawn mists, try to discover what lived hidden beneath all that water. The beavers thwacked their tails at my approach; the loons rolled their mournful calls out across the water.

Every few years, these small trips were replaced by the big ones. Besides the trip to the Tetons, one summer my parents hauled us into Colorado, Rocky Mountain National Park. There were car breakdowns, car sickness, stifling heat across the plains, but when the mountains rose up beyond Denver, I could hardly stand the rest of the drive to get into them. We took a ranger-guided hike to the top of Long's Peak, led by Ferrel Atkins, the park's version, I'm guessing, of Sage, and though his talk and leadership were mesmerizing, I chafed at the crowd of us, this herd of sheep struggling up to the heights.

I'm sure I was a model citizen, ever more sullen about being part of a society, of a family, and perhaps it was here that my father chased me around the hammock, dying to instill a little group ethic, but at some point during the trip, they granted my wish, happily, I'm sure, and left me and my spinning rod beside a little stream and drove off for another guided hike, promising to pick me up later in the afternoon. Alone at last, I edged through the long grass to the water, a pristine meandering stream, surrounded by mountains, the clear water we all marveled over after the tannin rust and coffee color of Wisconsin's waters. Eventually, casting the Rapala minnow I used with such lethality back home, I caught a little trout. But it was a trout. The fabled fish. My first ever. I wished the station wagon, the car with my parents, my brothers and sisters, would never return.

Or, earlier, when my mom's sister returned from years of missionary work in Peru, landing in a convent in Miami, their mother flew us all down to Florida for Christmas, a trip I remember only for a house they rented in the Keys, a deep-sea charter my father hired, for me, I'm sure, though I think my brothers joined in. But, again, all the tours, the guided hikes, left me crabbing for solitude, and somehow my parents overlooked the risk, or maybe relished it. Driving off with the rest of the family, they left me to wade and tumble and snorkel along an island coast for an afternoon, inspect the mangroves up close, giving in to an obsession they couldn't understand, something that could have led straight to child services.

It's been years and years, decades, since I've really recalled any of these trips, since that chafing to be away, to be alone in the wild, has ever come to mind. Maybe my call to them about going into Indian Creek never really came as quite the surprise I'd thought it had. But now, awake and looking out the window into the absolute pitch black of a rainy night in the wilderness, it all comes back, and I realize it wasn't just one thing or two, not a rocket launched or a salmon-egg job taken: it's been a lifetime leading me here. My parents opening the doors, allowing one of their litter to go feral. Maybe even my paper route was part of it, more than a thousand hours over the years of carrying weight around a hiked loop, my head free to wander, dreaming up all kinds of fantastic adventures.

Once, in Sylvania, probably about fifteen years old, my twin, Paul, sat up through most of a night, wracked with gut pain, my parents up with him. A few years before, he'd sledded into a tree, lost a kidney, his spleen, and already once since then he'd had to return to the hospital, scar tissue growing rampant, blocking and twisting his intestines. They knew the symptoms, knew they were miles and miles of lakes, two portages, from the car.

Predawn, without bothering with breaking camp, doing anything that would take time, we slid the canoes into the black water, eased Paul into the bottom, and set off paddling. I can't remember how we got him over the portages, only that we got him to the car, my dad driving to a tiny, rural hospital, and from there my mom and Paul flew out in a single-engine plane, more surgery, another long recovery. But I knew none of that, only that my wild sister, Terry, and I had been chosen to stay behind, to paddle back to camp, pack everything up, canoe back alone, meet my father at some vague point in the future.

The details are lost to me—how we met again with my father, how much time passed—only the turning back remains, pointing the bow of that canoe into the wilderness.

27

Bob Marshall Wilderness, Montana
May 2004

Giving up on the shade logs as the most hopeless kind of optimism, I toss them back into the dripping woods. I stand back, watching the rain dimple the open black water of each bucket, making them seem oddly vulnerable, exposed to the elements. I dig through the saddles and see a few fry swimming above the gravel and guess the rest are down in the rocks. Or maybe they've been swimming out all along without my catching them at it. There's no way to tell.

I walk past the reading tree day after day, the rain pelting down, the wind slanting it in at a 45. The salad days of the reading tree and hammock swings seem an awfully long time ago, an era I'm sure couldn't have lasted only a day or two. Marching back, I try to recall it precisely. There must have been nearly a week of sunny weather, but I can't really believe it.

The last week falls into a pattern: up at dawn, poking my head out the door, forty degrees, fifteen-mile-an-hour wind, rain, perking coffee on the woodstove, hoping for a lull to make the grayling loop. One morning, I dig out a scone mix, one of Nolan's favorites. Scattering flour on the cutting board, I knead the dough, puffing little white clouds into the air. Cranberry-orange scones. Jim Bridger and Hugh Glass rolling in their graves, flipping cartwheels.

I even crack Rose's minibottle of Bailey's, stashed in my pack with the Jiffy Pop, pour some into my coffee. Nailing down their coffin lids.

The radio calls for nothing but rain, thunderstorms, winds increasing to forty miles an hour. I stare out the window, coffee in one hand, hot scone in the other, and take a sip, throw another log into the stove.

By nine, staying dry and warm seems a low ambition, and, stuffed with scones, I crawl into yesterday's mud-caked clothes and set out. The first thing I run across, on the hill just above the cabin, are bear tracks, coming into the park. They follow the trail all the way from the falls and are almost half a foot across the front toes, claw marks more than an inch out in front, the straight-edged front footpad. Grizzly. I wonder how many hours ago. At least not heading my way. Today.

At Spruce Creek I make the stunning discovery of three fry swimming near the surface of the bucket, straining away from the pull of the exit spout every time they come within its reach. "Lewis! Clark! Sacagawea!" I shout. My bold explorers.

I start toward Biggs, armed with this new hope, the trail

up the hill away from the pack bridge so muddy that even ground-squirrel tracks are visible, down to every toe pad and claw mark. Before I reach the top of the hill, however, I see a new track, a first, but unmistakable. Wolf. Three and a half inches across, four-plus long, claw marks out front. Unlike the bear's, these tracks head downstream, my way, and I follow them along, my smile growing, stepping carefully to avoid rubbing them out.

The tracks stick to the trail, right past the pitching pond, where I stop and go through the motion, firing another stone into the water. Low and outside. The wolf tracks lead me down the Hill of Doom, even the wolf slipping and sliding.

I cross the halfway-point creek, following the wolf prints all the way. Then up the last hill to Biggs Flat.

A loner, the wolf keeps a steady pace, not veering off the trail once. I follow across the flats, down the slide to the creek. I leave it to cross over on my tree and pick it up again as soon as I regain the trail, still heading south, forging on. I say, "Well, good luck. Wherever you're going."

Dozens of swimmers top every bucket. I smile down, things happening.

After getting back up to the flats, I detour east, following the rim of the Biggs Creek cut. An enormous beaver complex piles up the water, a two-tiered dam spanning the valley, six feet high, at least a hundred yards long, bulged downstream.

I cross through some burn, more recent than most, the ground still black in spots, eventually coming out in the uppermost reaches of the flats. There, alone in the grass, is a massive aspen, mostly alive, bracketed by the skeletons of two others knocked flat, one still trying to send up vertical shoots, the other long dead and charred black. As I marvel at their size, the wind picks up, bringing the hike's first real rain. The aspen leaves rustle, one of the best sounds in the world, even better out here in the open than held in by the thick groves of white trunks and silver-green leaves.

The rain lashes down, and I head out, keeping my elevation for a while before giving in, angling back down toward the trail, picking it up again just before the halfway creek.

Crossing the bridge, the river clear despite all the rain—the heat and snowmelt apparently bringing it up more than just rain—I hike the bear trail from the bridge to Gates, singing my lungs out. No more sign of my track maker, though.

The day still nasty and low, blowing and spitting rain and sleet, I open the cabin, glad to get out of it for a bit. I work into evening making wooden knives for the boys, leather sheathes, struggling to break the ivories out of an elk skull to add to their bundles. By the time I finish, I've got saws involved, spikes, hammers. I break one ivory, cut the hell out of myself. Too wet to go out, and too cold to play ball. So we sat in the house. We did nothing at all.

By late evening the wind dies down, and though the clouds to the west are still dramatic, they've lifted a little, and I spot an actual patch of blue. About the size of a dime, but still. The clouds close over it, but soon there's a new one. Maybe another.

By nightfall, I spot a couple of stars, only a few, and far between, but real stars. Still up there after all.

28

Bob Marshall Wilderness, Montana
May 2004

A dozen elk blow out from in front of the bunkhouse as I open the cabin door. Even after seeing the same kind of thing almost every day, it stops me cold: the flurry of motion, the charge onto the runway, the slow to a trot, then the turn and stop, assessing me, the threat. Then, after a minute or so, a head either tossed back, a cow leading the group into the trees, or dropping down, grazing resumed.

As the cabin warms, I munch through a few stale scones, and, having used a total of one of the eggs I'd brought in, I take a trip down to the root cellar, spooking the elk again, and make myself a scramble. Even after breakfast it's only thirty-seven degrees, the overcast solid, the wind light, the rain just barely holding back. The radio claims the weather will be beautiful by Wednesday. I'm leaving Tuesday.

I grease my boots for the day's trek, pack the pack, throwing in fishing gear. My only real chore at the buckets is to peer into them, see if anything's swimming around. But that, I have to admit, is pretty much what my job has been all along.

At the pitching pond, I spot a big, brown, neckless mass rooting about in the burn, and my heart charges. I whisper, "Come on, lift your head, lift your head, prove you're not a bear." There's something not quite right about it, but I search the forest of burned-naked trunks for something to climb. Then the brown mass of rain-streaked hair lifts not one head, but two, a pair of elk, down in some hole, their legs hidden. Soon ten more lift their heads, stand slowly up out of their beds.

I'd found a good pitching stone a quarter of a mile earlier, and I heft it in my hand, wrap my thumb and first two fingers around it, shift it, four seam, two seam, curve. I've done my best not to interrupt things: the elk on the airstrip, the whiteys around the cabin, the robin in her nest. The elk watch. I find my place, lift my hands to my chest, raise my leg. The elk hold, and slowly I lower my leg, let my stone fall. For tomorrow. I move on down the Hill of Doom, the mud hardening around the wolf tracks I'd been careful to avoid walking over, saving them, too.

After crossing the bridge tree, a fresh coyote track stands out in the trail, almost laughably small beside the wolf's. A few steps farther on, brand-new bear tracks. Five inches across the rounded footpad, and where the claws show at all, they're only a half an inch beyond the toes. A good-size black bear. I raise my voice, waiting to see a bear in midstream, gorging on my tiny fry.

But the only thing I find in the incubators are a few

more swimmers circling near the top. And a few dollops of white bird poop on the saddles. A dipper in here could reduce a population in a hurry, but the last thing I'd ever do is shoot a dipper. My fish are already nothing but prey.

Back up top, though the weather doesn't exactly call for it, I stop at the reading tree and pull out Nick and an apple. I make it through an apple's worth of "Big Two-Hearted River," one of my favorites, but the wind's driving out of the north, and I have to finally admit that I'm shivering, the book trembling in my hand. I pull my raincoat's zipper to my chin, shove my hands in my pockets, and march hard, reheating.

At Spruce Creek, the hair still marking the calf's spot in the Hansel and Gretel stretch, there are no swimmers above the saddles in the first buckets, but the last is swarming with them. While I watch, several get flushed out the exit spout, off on their big adventure, life. I whisper, "Bon voyage," but, still, it's hardly a mass exodus. With complete RSI removal scheduled for two days, I tell the fish they'd best get it in gear.

In the log, I note that the bucket with the movers and shakers has fewer biosaddles than any of the others, wondering if there's a connection. Maybe things in there are just a little too tenement-like, the fish tiring of it more quickly, the competition for space too tough. I suggest screens for the buckets once the lids are removed, keeping out the dippers. Things for Lee and Dave to ponder over the winter.

After carrying my fly rod all day, I finally fish the Sun just half a mile above the pack bridge. Quickly breaking down to nymphing, I catch one more of the Sun's fabled cut-bows, the rainbow-cutthroat cross dooming the native cut-throats.

Up the trail to the park, singing "Take Me Out to the Ball Game" one more time, I cross new wolf tracks a quarter of a mile from the cabin. A pair this time, both smaller than the one that went down to Biggs, one smaller than the other. A female and a youngster?

At the cabin, thinking about horse loads, I gather all my stuff together and pack up one dry bag for good, get the rest of my stuff a little more organized, mostly fill the second pack, leaving free some clothes, my day pack and rain gear, bear spray and revolver. Then, sprucing up for company, my homecoming, I take a last shower, mainly because I think I should, rather than any great desire to again face the wind naked and wet.

Finger-combing my hair, I flip on the radio and make a last effort, asking them to relay the message that the fish aren't ready. They put me on hold, then come back, saying Tom and Dave will be coming in on Monday, as planned. I acknowledge and drop the mic down to the desk, look around the cabin, home.

I poke through dinner until I notice shadows on the table. I do a double-take, then step out to stare, struggling to re-call the sun's last appearance. Ducking back in just long enough to grab my fly rod, I stumble into the willow thick-ets of Gates, heading, at last, for the beaver pond.

On my way up, I catch cutthroats, purebloods, at almost every place I cast. They all seem bigger than before, the

sunshine working its wonders. I work my way to the base
of the dam and again stand there for a moment. But this
time, I step up, picking my footing over the fretwork of
sticks, and, at long last, I stand atop the dam, water flowing
over my shoes, down the face below me. A huge pond
stretches motionless, the hump of a beaver lodge out toward
the middle, the water shallower, reedier between it and the
left edge of the pond. It's everything I'd imagined, and after
another moment, I cast, stretching way out, letting it fly, the
whole line. My fly touches down and sits quietly while the
ripples die out around it. Nothing. At all. I feel kind of fool-
ish, watching it dead and flat, with none of a creek's rush
giving it any action. I start stripping back for another try,
and wham. A full eight inches of cutthroat, a leviathan. Like
bluegills, or bass, they fall one after another for the fly stripping across the water.

A beaver surfaces, spotting me and swimming closer to
inspect. Only thirty feet away, it stops, floating and watching, its eyes impossibly black, the wet fur clumped, its head
low, body like a chunk of driftwood behind it. It edges
toward me until I shift my weight. That's too much, and it
dives with the rifle-shot-warning thwack of its tail, one of
my favorite sounds from childhood, that and the calls of
loons stretching across the flat water of Wisconsin lakes.
I stand on the dam grinning.

Working back onto shore, I find a new stretch of water
to try up toward the head of the pond, trout dimpling the
surface. Upstream, five elk cross the neck of the pond, dropping down to their bellies, then lurching back up onto the
grassy bank, water streaming from their flanks. I stand in

the long shadow of a lone pine, and they don't make me out, only stare down toward me for a while, step closer, nose up, testing the air, then give up and go back to their feeding.

Three beaver come out, cutting broad Vs through the water. Without my casting, they swim within feet, peering at me with their marble-black eyes, twitching rubbery noses. One dives, surfacing again only a second later, a few feet closer. It shakes the water off its head, leaving it with a punk do. No tail slapping this time, they swim off together toward the dam. The sky fills with the winnowing of the snipe, diving and swooping, laying their claims.

This is the evening that every challenge with the boys would have been worth. No, they couldn't have made the Biggs hike day after day. There were days I felt I couldn't. And I couldn't have held them close enough through the Hansel and Gretel stretch. I couldn't have left them alone at the cabin for hours straight either. A bear in the trail would have made me rue the day I'd been fool enough to put them at such risk, would have brought out the sick, chilly sweat, the flip of my stomach, the cold, scorching realization that I'd done something dumb with the two people I always have to be smart about. But this, the gold evening light, the new snow on Beartop dipping below tree line, the beaver so close, checking out this new thing, much the same way the boys would have, the snipe filling the air—maybe this is what they'd have brought out of here. Maybe the rest of it, the hard stuff, the rain, the bears, would have turned them into lifelong city dwellers, though in my experience the hard stuff is what you remember best, what you look back at knowing you'd done something. But maybe even this night would, in the end, provide them only an entertaining anecdote for their future cocktail parties. "Well, my lunatic father once dragged us into the middle of the wilderness for a month. We were hardly more than babies. He walked the legs off of us, every day trudging through the rain, dodging grizzly bears, to stare into some black buckets of fish eggs. Then, as a treat, he'd drag us to this pond reeking of beaver shit and tilt our heads up to the sky and say, 'Listen to the snipe!' "

Someone would laugh, say, "There really isn't such a thing as a snipe, is there? Isn't that just a joke? Going snipe hunting?"

And maybe they'd laugh it all off, say, "I have no idea."

But maybe this would have given them their rocket to chase, their Indian Creek, their Sylvania or mangrove swamp, their steep Colorado valley. Now, they would never know, I would never know, and that's the district ranger's unforgivable sin. Sure, he'd been right, accidentally, but now we'll never know. And isn't the risk worth it, to give them that chance to find out?

Those chances. It's all, everything leading me here, been so accidental. My father pointing me into a pond. Rader at a keg, crushed on some girl he'd hardly ever see again. One too many body recoveries in a lake I never thought I'd see. A girl walking up to my lifeguard chair, telling me about a job babysitting salmon. A supervisor who would believe anything I wrote down on his river application. The great good luck of a broken shoulder putting me under Sage's tutelage. But, really, isn't it all that way? Just one thing leading to the next, to the next? I mean, does anyone actually plan this stuff?

And, good god, if they did, who could have possibly imagined such a string of pure chance? Who could have had such hope?

I cast again, strip in another cutthroat, and the sun sinks behind the mountains at my back, the air chilling. I break down my fishing rod and slog onto higher ground, cut through the band of trees on my way back to the cabin.

The boys' time will come. They'd been denied this chance, but their time, and their chances, will come.

29

Bob Marshall Wilderness, Montana
May 2004

Mʸ last day alone. The rain starts again in the night, the thermometer dipping to one degree above freezing. As more light seeps into the sky, I see that the overcast is at least higher. Despite the drizzle, it doesn't have that completely socked-in Seattle feel, the worry that I am beginning to look like a cave fish.

I climb the hill in a spatter of rain, but by the time I reach the bridge, I take my raincoat off. I tie it around my waist instead of stuffing it into my pack, easier to get it back on, but only have to hustle into it twice before reaching Biggs.

At the buckets, I find a few dozen swimmers above the saddles, staying steadfastly away from the outflow. Nobody in any hurry. I say, "Last chance, guys. Tomorrow, the hook."

Though the rain slacks off, the wind on the flats rips along. I stay in the shelter of the creek for lunch, reading a little more Ernie, resting up before braving the wind, the hike home. My last, I suppose. Tomorrow, Tom will probably make me get on a horse.

I soldier home, trying to see everything this last time, remember which big dug-out hole was the badger's, finding the best still-visible wolf tracks. My last hike through the Hansel and Gretel stretch is not one I'll miss, and all's the same at the Spruce Creek incubators. I claw up the hill one more time, the seemingly inexhaustible supply of soot still streaking my hands and shins black.

It's not until I'm back at Gates that the sun breaks through for real. Though the hammock is buried at the bottom of the Duluth pack, which is at the very bottom of my one completely packed dry bag, I empty everything to retrieve it and set it up in its old spot at the edge of the airstrip. I even step through the half door of the root cellar, liberating the lone beer Tom and Dave left behind a month ago. Swinging in the hammock, I have an evening toast to the park. As pleasant as it is, the regret of leaving and the anticipation of seeing the boys and Rose tinges the edges.

The hammock—my dad's navy berth. They dropped the atom bombs on Hiroshima and Nagasaki while he was still in the navy's radio and radar school in Chicago. At the time, he'd been disappointed to have missed it all, not shipping out to the Philippines until November, moving to shore on a landing craft. Only then, imagining machine-gun bullets ringing against the steel door that was about to drop open, did he think that maybe he'd been lucky. If it hadn't been for the extra year of radar training, he would have been at Okinawa, beneath the cloud of kamikazes. Eager to get home, he declined the navy's offer to stay and observe the nuclear tests at Kwajalein, though he'd been interested. Which probably kept me from being born with two heads.

All such close calls. Rose's dad running down ice-filled irrigation ditches, hiding from German tanks. My dad born six months to the right side of a timeline. I remembered a book tour bringing me back to Milwaukee three months before Nolan was born, taking a run with my parents out into the Wisconsin countryside, to Horicon Marsh, a famous birding spot we'd been to several times when I was a kid. Walking the trails through the sumac, cattails, and milkweed, talking about this new thing on my horizon, children, my dad offhandedly mentioned that having kids was the best thing that had ever happened in his life.

Sitting in his hammock, I remember my stunned surprise at that revelation. His sole ambition as a kid had been to be a navy pilot. But hay fever had kept him from that, and after the war the GI bill got him an engineering degree, and he'd gotten married and had kids. He never had any great love for engineering, he said, but it was a good way to support his family. As a young man, I'd been unable to believe anyone would work at something they didn't enjoy. Just for a family. And the whole long drive back out to Montana, I wondered what it was that took me so far away from my parents, and whether, once they were gone, it would have seemed worth it, all those years apart, if I'd even be able to recall what had made it seem so necessary at the time. I replayed that one line in my head, hearing him say we were the best thing in his life. A big man, one who slightly scared my childhood friends, never overly demonstrative, such statements were not something he littered through conversations.

One of our great recreations as kids was a game he invented called Mean Man. Our mother and sisters sequestered in their rooms, we'd turn off all the lights in the house, stuff light-blocking towels beneath their doors. Then my brothers and I snuck through the darkened house, attacking him with our pillows, getting snared in his arms, tickled while he squeezed tighter and tighter, until we couldn't breathe, couldn't squeak out any sound at all, and then a long moment more before he'd toss us aside and grab his next victim. That's the kind of game Big Dan came up with. My boys were as dying to play it as we had been.

I lie back in the hammock, the elk coming out, unable to recognize me as anything at all. The mosquitoes begin to whine, the clouds to build. Seventy-eight years old, one quadruple bypass under his belt already, odds are I won't have my father to kick around a lot longer, and I wonder, fifty years from now, rocking in the hammock of their long dead and gone and barely remembered grandpa, what they'd think about my life. Or if I'd ever be able to do anything more than bore them by saying what I hoped would be the most obvious thing I could ever say, that they were the best things that had ever happened in my life.

I tilt myself out of the hammock, turn back into a two-legged creature, the most dangerous on the planet, and the elk retreat to the airstrip's far edge. I untie the hammock, fold it, brushing away every pine needle.

After dinner, I break out one of Aidan's Jiffy Pops, reading the instructions with too much attention, shuffling the aluminum foil pan carefully across the top of the wood-stove. The onion bulb of foil grows, popcorn plinking off it, driving it outward in hundreds of tiny dents, and when it seems finished I sit down at the table, opening the foil with the point of my fillet knife. I toss a couple of steaming kernels into my mouth. Without Rose and the boys to go back to, I'd find a way to spend the summer here. Volunteer for trail crew. Something. In the beginning, I'd thought it would be great to walk someplace new now and then, but, forced to walk the same route day after day after day, I've gotten to see and know one small piece of this world. Nothing but the egg duties would have forced me into something that repetitive—in my backpacking days I'd taken drastic measures to assure not having to return on the same trail I'd taken out—but I've learned the elks' haunts, their response to me, saw that it wasn't all chance, that they had their favorite spots, even within such a tight area. The repetition, instead of blinding me to all else, has opened my eyes to much more than I would have otherwise known.

But within a week or two this place will be crawling with trail crews, wilderness guards, outfitters, backpackers, horse packers, firefighters. In the spring at Indian Creek, I'd taken pains to avoid the first people coming in to the river, and I wonder how many evenings like this I'd have at the cabin. I picture evening after evening lurking by the creek, hiding in the willows, hopelessly willing everyone to go away.

No, I've been fortunate to have the place to myself, and I'm equally fortunate to be leaving at the right time, however hard the leaving is.

I move out for one last go at the beaver ponds, but while I'd sat wondering, the storms had stacked up in earnest over the mountains, the sky heading early toward night. I reach back in for my raincoat and step into the first curls of wind. Maybe, just maybe, this one will shoot by to the north.

The beaver pond, wind-riffled but not white-capped, is about as perfect a place as I've ever found. I stand on the dam, the water pouring across my toes, and watch the beaver trio come over to inspect me again, leaving with a lone tail slap.

There are a lot of fish, and I catch the champ of the day, of the whole trip, a bona fide ten-incher, all rusty gill plates and crimson throat slash. As he swims away, I drop the fly in front of him, and he turns briefly, giving it a thought before continuing down to the black depths.

Two beaver reappear, swimming toward one another until they stop nose to nose. They circle each other that way, noses touching, a yin-and-yang pattern rippling the pond. A first flurry of raindrops pocks the water; then the entire surface blurs with overlapping rings. Hopping from tussock to tussock, avoiding the beaver channels, having long ago had too much cold experience with how deep they can be, I run straight into three giant stalks of elephant's head.

I stop dead, rain hammering my hood. I smile maybe the widest I have yet. I remember so clearly finding these for the first time in the Tetons, pioneering a new channel, Half Moon, pulling my raft over a tight spot, and stumbling into these flowers, tall stalks covered with perfect pink facsimiles of elephant heads, wide flapping ears, broad forehead, long, up-curled trunk. I rushed down the rest of the channel, the rest of the trip, snagged Rose away from her lettuce-shredding job at Colter Bay, got her out on the river that evening, down the same almost-dead-end channel, revealing this perfect treasure. They were so precisely shaped, so perfectly named, so perfectly ours that I was disappointed to see them in a wildflower guide, almost unwilling to believe that they'd already been discovered, named, known to others.

As I sit staring, remembering, the rain slashes down at angles hard to believe. I leapfrog through the sage for the cabin, but, before I get the door shut behind me, the sun breaks through, the rain still smoking down. I turn away from the cabin, stand out in the driving rain, the golden light, the very air alive. The storm passes toward Beartop, a double rainbow arcing after it, every blade and needle and twig glittering.

As the light fails, I step inside, grab up a handful of already-stale popcorn, and can't stop smiling.

30

After the evening show, I wake the next morning to nothing but another solid overcast, thirty degrees, clouds scooting east, elk at the corrals, deer just outside the window. I start the fire, the coffee. In the dim light, I finish my packing, wanting it all set for Tom, only leaving out my day's clothes, sleeping bag, and toothbrush. On the bench beneath the nails that I've hung my pack and coat on all month, I set out my rain gear and camera, binos and water bottle for the saddlebags. At the very top of the blue dry bag, I layer in the boys' savage wear and medicine bags, knives and moccasins, ready to retrieve them at the trailhead.

With every strap tightened, I fetch the spring scale from the bunkhouse and hang it from a spike in one of the cabin's rafter logs. Each pack weighs in at sixty pounds. At ten o'clock, after reloading the wood box, the kindling bucket, sweeping and mopping, I take my day pack and bear spray, leaving my revolver packed away, and head out for my last hike down to Biggs. I'll be early for our noon meeting but guess that Tom and Dave will be too—nothing much I can think of that would hold them at Cabin Creek till midday.

As if a parting gift, I find a new set of bear tracks at the top of the hill above the cabin, heading toward the bridge, just like me. They're big but have curved footpads and hardly discernable claw marks. A black. I follow along, glad I have a relatively late start, that the bear will be well on his way to wherever it is they go for the day. But I sing away, bringing "Goober Peas" out of the mothball pile and finally remembering the tune of "Ode to Joy," which has escaped me the last few days.

Belting that out, I clear the dark timber of bear alley and step into a stiff breeze in the open, empty burn, the drop down to the river. The clouds, narrow gaps beginning to split through here and there, race along, something to watch all on their own. At the last steep turn, looking down at the trail to keep from breaking my neck, I spin through the hairpin, sliding across the loose gravel and dirt, and come face-to-butt with the bear making the tracks I've been following.

Less than ten yards ahead of me, the bear becomes aware of me at the same instant. Instead of bolting, dashing across the bridge, it rears around, standing up to face me. For a moment he hangs there, the two of us face-to-face, his eyes small in his big, black, glossy head.

After that instant's hesitation, the bear follows through his whirling spin, falling back to his front feet, his hind legs kicking into gear, launching into a rolling bound off the trail, following the little footpath downriver, the same path I'd used to reach the fishing hole at the bend below the bridge.

With the wind, the rush and tumble of the river, we'd had no chance of hearing each other, no matter how loudly I sang. I remember to take a breath.

The bear follows the trail for only a few seconds, thirty yards maybe, before veering toward the river, crashing through the brush, headlong into the water. I make my own legs work at last, sliding down the hill, dashing onto the bridge.

The full current hits the bear, sweeping it downstream another thirty yards before it regains its footing, claws its way into the narrow shallows on the other bank, barreling up the improbably steep face of the hill, toward the trail that climbs up out of the river bottom on its way toward Biggs.

A little more than halfway up to the trail, the bear stops, twisting around to look at me, as if *I* might be chasing *it*. A head-to-tail shake sends a halo of river water away from his midnight coat. Then he fires out a tremendous load of shit. Remembering how we'd just stood there staring at each other, me using the one second I had before he'd charge not to reach for my bear spray, or look for a tree, or do anything at all but gape, I can't help but whisper, "I know how you feel."

The bear lunges the last few chugging yards up to the trail, then turns down it, heading south, the same direction I have to go. "No," I shout, "not that way!" and, surprisingly enough, he stops, turning to look over his shoulder at me. I point east and he lumbers off trail in that direction, climbing the rest of the hill, disappearing in the bristle of black, limbless lances that used to be pines. I stand on the bridge several minutes, thinking, "Man speaks to bear. Bear listens," still not quite able to believe I'd frozen the way I had. After weeks imagining just such a meeting, I hadn't even thought of the bear spray.

All my thoughts from the other night at the beaver pond, the risk being worth whatever the boys would have taken away, wither in the face of that bear. How much of a deterrent would Aidan, probably out front, charging ahead as ever, have seemed? Would the bear have turned and fled or seen a snack bumping right up against him? I would have charged then, but to what use? And what about Nolan then? What was worth this risk? What had my parents thought when they got that call, "I'll be out of touch the next seven months, living in a tent in the wilderness"? But I'd been taking that risk myself. And I was twenty. Immortal. Choosing to bring the boys in would have been my choice, not theirs. They wanted to go, begged to, but I was the only one who knew the risks entailed.

I step across the rest of the bridge and start up the hill. Finding the damp footprints in the trail, I stall, searching the blackened snags for the bear, not, after watching him dash away, expecting to see him, but not wanting to bump into him again after having demonstrated how dangerously quick-witted I am.

I cross the tiny creek and over the hills to the pond. The wind moans through the snags, an odd, mournful whistling, as I find the stone I dropped yesterday and go full windup and let fly.

I stop at the reading tree, linger a moment there beneath the branches, surveying my realm, the long stretch of grass and wildflowers down to the burn, the river hidden, but the green rise of the mountains showing where it lies.

When I reach the drop into Biggs, I make out horses standing in my lunch spot, the same place Tom and I'd tied up when we'd met Lee the first day. I drop down the hill, wishing I had a last tour of the eggs to myself.

Tom spots me as I reach the creek, gives a wave as I head down to the crossing log and then over it, up the trail into the trees, crossing the backwater slough on another log, past yesterday's bear tracks, and into the opening with the horses and Tom. We shake hands, smiling, and I wonder if, after that kick to the head, he remembers me at all.

Dave's down in the creek, the lower incubators already emptied and taken apart, a pile of PVC piping and connections, some empty gravel baskets, the streambed full of churned-up mud. He looks up at me with a grin. "Lots of fry still here," he says. And though he seems pleased, I say, "Yeah, I don't think they'd really started to leave on their own."

He nods, points at big groups of fry holding in any spot of quiet water in the trickle of the spring creek. "Looks great. Hardly any dead eggs in any of these."

He lurches out of the sucking mud, comes up the cutbank, and shakes my hand. We walk upstream, and I tell my latest bear story, only an hour old.

Tom blanches, stops me, asks me to repeat it, asks where it happened. "Should have left a satellite phone with you. Pain to carry, but . . ."

"What? Easy for the bear to digest?"

He shakes his head. "Bad place to be alone," he says, and waves us on toward the upstream buckets.

Dave reaches in, scooping handful after handful of biosaddles out of the forty-six-degree water, piling them into an old feed bag. I start doing the same in the other bucket, offering Dave one of my neoprene gloves. He declines, saying he guesses he's already caught all the arthritis he can hold. I wear mine, guessing arthritis can always get worse and knowing I've pushed it about as hard as anyone possibly could.

The gravel beneath the saddles swarms with fry. I ask Dave about Lee's instructions, how important he said it was to operate the incubators until all the fish leave on their own. He shrugs. "At most it lets them put on a little more size. That's the only advantage. These guys will be fine."

As we work, lifting out the gravel tray, letting most of the fry out, then tipping the buckets to wash the most reluctant into the wild, Tom sees something darting in the pool beneath us. He walks out onto the prickly spruce snag lying across the pool, its longest branches dragging into the water. "Brook trout," he says, like a death sentence.

Dave jerks up. "Those meat-eating sons of bitches!"

Half a dozen little trout, the white leading edges of their fins making them easy to spot, slice through the stream of defenseless fry we've just created.

In all my time walking up this channel I've never spotted a fish. We guess they've followed the trail of early departees up to the mother lode. We step into the creek, hoping to haze the fish out, but our every step stirs up clouds of silt, blinding us to the slaughter.

Leaving the grayling to chance, and brook trout, we move back to the horses, following the spring, finding fry holding all along the creek, even in the big slough the trail crosses. Dave talks about putting up signs, warning horse packers of a grayling crossing.

We've spent a full two hours dismantling the incubators, wrestling brook trout, and, as Tom packs the awkward lengths of pipe onto Molly, he gets on Dave about the time. "We're only halfway there. I didn't know you were going to personally say good-bye to every single fish."

Dave ignores him, too busy looking for a stump or rock he can use to jump-start his ascent of his horse, Tucker. "You know what *that* rhymes with," he grumbles. I ask why he, as less than the world's tallest guy, has gotten paired with the biggest horse I've seen. "Seventeen and a half hands high," he marvels, but then shrugs. "He's a department horse."

Tom mounts up. I reintroduce myself to Gus. Dave finds a log and hauls himself up as if crawling over battlements.

We set out. No more hiking for me.

The quick ride up to Spruce Creek is, though, really a joy. Not having to watch my feet, I'm able to rubberneck, point out different things I've seen while they've been gone.

I show them the wolf tracks coming down the Hill of Doom, though I don't share the hill's name. We pass the pitching pond, almost in sight of the bridge. Tom, leading the way, pulls off the trail with his pack string, lets me and Dave go past. "We'll have a battle on our hands, keeping them going past home, holding them there while Dave shakes hands with six thousand grayling. You two go on ahead, and I'll take the string up to Gates, get them corralled, then come back with Molly to pack up the incubators."

We don't have time to argue but ride ahead as instructed, me in the lead, sitting that much straighter on Gus, waiting for his revolt when we bypass the bridge. I tell myself to jump toward the hill side of the trail, not the drop-off.

But Gus listens after only a few gentle heel nudges, a tug on the reins, and we ride past the bridge, Gus plodding through Headquarters Creek, picking his way, but behind me I hear scuffling, a few rapid hoof beats, then Dave rhyming at the top of his lungs, "Tucker you fucker!"

By the time I get turned around, Dave's on his feet, not on his horse. With Tucker's height, it's like dropping off a roof. Tugging at the reins, still rhyming his heart out, Dave slogs through the creek, pulling Tucker after him. He says, "No, he didn't buck me off. He started getting excited, crow-hopping, and I *chose* to get off."

"As long as it was your choice."

"Exactly."

We ride through the dark stuff, somehow safer off the ground, and tie the horses up tight above Spruce Creek, only half a foot of rope between nose and tree. They snort and neigh, Tucker bucking his head, pulling against the tree, but Dave has him on belay and finishes his hitch in between Tucker's lunges, rhyming the whole time.

Giving them a wide berth, we cross the trail and drop down to Spruce.

The fry here are much the same as at Biggs, about half

an inch long, swarming beneath the biosaddles, above the gravel, in no hurry to leave. We release them all out into the world, Dave noting the low sediment levels, wondering if a replacement site should be considered for Biggs.

He doesn't shake fins with each one, and soon we've got all the pipe and buckets and saddles hauled back up the hill to Tucker and Gus. As we sit waiting for Tom, the sun comes out, and pretty soon we're lying back, propped up on elbows, watching the sun touch the river.

Maybe an hour later, Tom rides up, leading Molly, and we push ourselves up with groans, giving him a hard time about being late. He ignores us, tying up, then reaches into Molly's pannier to throw my muck boots to me.

"Those will come in handy now."

He holds out the feed sack we packed the biosaddles into, and I take it, saying, "Now that we actually could use."

"I bet," he answers.

Inside, instead of biosaddles, is a six-pack of beer, one ring empty.

So we all sit back down in the green grass, the lowering sun. There aren't yet six empty rings when we're startled by a sudden rush and commotion in the brush, and before we've done anything more than sit up straight, Tom's mule, the infamous Pete, thunders into our midst.

Tom laughs. "That thick-headed mule. He just can't stand being away from Molly. He must have jumped the corral."

Dave assesses the dripping-wet mule. "Looks like he swam the river, too."

Tom nods. "He's never cared much for bridges."

We drain the last of the beer and load Molly, tie a lead rope onto Pete, and ride the last stretch downriver and across to Gates, the sun setting.

Tom offers to take care of the horses if we start dinner, but not until he's inspected the corral, found a cracked top rail, the telltale patch of Pete's black hair. "Darn mule's got legs like a moose," he says.

Dave snags the grill out of the bunkhouse and another feeding frenzy ensues: eight steaks, three pork chops, potatoes, salad. "The pork chops are left over from last night," Dave says.

With dinner at nine o'clock, it's a short night; a few stories, Tom's questions about my school career, asking who I knew from those days, make it clear he remembers nothing of the ride in. He says he slept thirteen hours straight when he got home after that trip and felt much better when he woke up. With a stretch, Dave says he'll take his snoring out to the bunkhouse, and Tom and I settle in, the lantern dying out, the whitewashed rafter logs glowing for a second in its aftermath. No moon, it's just as dark outside as in.

The boys. Tomorrow.

31

Tom and I are quiet as we light the lantern, start the coffee. Following routine, he volunteers to get the horses lined out while I handle the cooking. We step out into a steady drizzle. Even in the predawn dark, we can see fresh snow down to the park.

He turns up his collar, stopping at the bunkhouse long enough to roll out Dave, then disappears into the dark and the rain.

I turn back into the hissing lantern light and stoke the fire, mix pancake batter, add the can of blueberries Tom set out, pour hot water into the boxes of dried hash browns, set the biggest cast iron skillet on the stove, and load it with sausage. Tom has a dozen fresh eggs, wrapped in newspaper, the way I've learned it's done for horse packing.

Dave stumbles in, smiling, surveying the cooking scene.

"I'll take the sausage," he says. "Never have excelled at pancakes."

Cracking all the eggs into another skillet, I walk out past the bunkhouse, find Tom saddling horses, tell him it's time.

He says, "Right there," and I turn back, the light streaming into the dawn from the cabin windows, the smoke curling up, hanging low in the rain, the dusting of fresh white on the mountains behind it.

I set Tom's cup in front of his place, and as soon as he comes through the door, we pull up the benches and start shoveling breakfast in like it's a job.

After only a minute to catch our breath, I carry out my packs for Tom to mantee. While they pack, I give the cabin a last mopping, a last setting of everything in its place. The shutters have to be bolted this time, and I shove the ten-inch bolts through their holes, then go back in, the cabin gone dark and gloomy, damp with the mopping. I have to use a flashlight to see enough to twist the nuts down tight.

That done, every last duty I can think of, I step out to the hitching rails. I offer help, but mostly only watch as Tom hefts the packs up onto the mules, does his rope tricks, gets everything set.

The ground cleared, I ask, "Ready for me to lock up?"

They are, and I walk back to the cabin. Instead of stepping inside wearing my muddy boots, I only poke my head in the door, check the stove, the table, my bed, make sure I've slid the window shut. One last look around. I lock the main door and walk around to the porch, blowing the robin out of her nest one last time, and lock that door. I give both locks a tug, kick a scraping of mud off the porch boards, and walk back to the horses.

Dave and Tom are already up, Tom holding the lead rope of the pack string. "Pete treat you all right this time?" I ask.

He smiles, nods.

"So, I'm not going to be hearing 'Pete, you son of a bitch' quite so much on this ride?"

"Up to you," he says.

I climb aboard Gus, and Tom says, "You two go ahead and lead."

Dave and I glance at each other, and I wonder if Tom just wants to see the action or if it's easier for him to ride along afterward to pick up survivors.

I nudge Gus forward, get him clomping through the thick mud up the hillside. The whitetail, as they have almost every morning, prance away, launching themselves skyward in their odd, meaningless leaps. Just before entering the trees, I turn to look back at the park, dim and heavily green, no elk on the airstrip yet, though I think I can feel them in the trees, glad to have the place to themselves again. The grizzly too, maybe.

I watch everything I've tromped past every day, my fishing holes, the bear tracks. I don't have to sing my way through bear alley, and I miss it, humming "Take Me Out to the Ball Game" quietly enough that Dave won't hear.

At the bridge, Tom nudges his horse around us, saying, "I don't know about the two of you, but I'd like to get home tonight." He gives a smile, and, watching the string clomp over the bridge, I ask Dave if he knows how to get the horses to step it out.

He only raises an eyebrow. "They know," he says.

So we fall in behind the string, then fall behind, Gus resuming his coming in trick, trotting, or dozing.

By Biggs the sky has started to open a little, and by the time we cross the creek, I've unzipped my raincoat. We pull into the usual tying-up spot, and while Tom balances loads, Dave and I check the creek for fry, finding them thick in the trail's backwater pool. The brook trout are still up high by the spruce snag, the water clear now. The grayling are just going to have to do their best. They have years of this ahead of them. Survival of the fittest. A lot of them, most of them, are nothing more than food.

We mount up, and Tom says, "Don't let them lag. They know what they're supposed to do."

The ride out is much the same as the ride in, only longer and shaded with a completely different kind of anticipation—a leaning toward the known rather than the unknown, home and love instead of wilderness, the wilds.

We ride and ride, hours' worth, and then more hours, and I get just as uncomfortable, more so, but I lean forward, urge Gus to keep up, my life waiting for me at the trailhead.

We climb the cliff face of the Lake Trail, pause at the sight of the wreck, the swimming horse, but push on, everyone anxious to reach the end. I know better than to look back again.

32

Gibson Reservoir, Montana
June 2004

It's late, almost five, and I can barely sit on the horse any-more when Tom at last lets me know we're near. I can see the little dock, the parking lot above it, and instead of look-ing for elk, for bears, I look only for the boys, knowing they'd be able to wait a lot longer than an hour if there are rocks to throw into water. But we're still too far to see the splashes, the floating sticks they'd throw in for targets.

The trail turns away from the lake, rising through grass and aspen and pine, passing a signpost pointing to the trail-head.

We drop out of the trees and onto a road. A paved road. Civilization. The horses clip-clop along the asphalt and Tom tells me to come up, to lead us into the parking lot. He wants Rose to see me first. I decline, not wanting to play at some-thing so false, me leading a group of horses anywhere but off a cliff, but Tom insists, and Gus, knowing exactly how close he is, loses his last shred of hesitation.

Tom tells me which way to go, and I lead the troop into the upper parking lot, instead of the lower. There aren't many trucks in either, a few here and there, and I aim toward the Fish and Game trucks, the horse trailer. In the lower lot there's a Forest Service rig, a long pale green horse trailer, and, behind it, I spot our truck, Rose sitting on the tailgate. I can't see the boys.

As we clatter across the lot, Rose looks up. I can't not grin, but I struggle not to look simply addled. I raise my hand, wave, and she waves back, not bothering to get up. Then I see Nolan, dodging into the outhouse. Glancing back at Rose, I see she's looking into the trees, probably trying to spot Aidan, the great disappearer.

I think she's taking the whole reunion pretty calmly, but I guide Gus up to the horse trailer that Tom points out. "Just tie him up to the side of the trailer," he says.

I do, not nearly so tired and sore anymore. A little fringe of trees and rocks hide the lower lot, and I walk around the trailer, step between the trees to see Rose still sitting on the tailgate.

I wave again, call her name. She stands up, surprised, and calls Aidan's name. She's facing away, but I hear her say, "Aidan, Dad's here. Aidan!"

A moment later, Aidan comes tearing out of the trees and Rose points. He dashes across the lower lot and through the trees, popping out just in front of me, looking up, then hesitates, studying my face.

My beard. I smile and take a knee, say, "It's me," and

hold out my arms. He jumps into them, buries his face in my neck and shoulder for just a second, then rears back to look at me again. "You look funny," he says.

"So do you," I say. "You always have." I hug him tight, and hear Nolan charging through the trees, yelling, "Dad!"

I catch his charge, too. He nearly strangles me in his hug. Then Rose. "You were too far away," she says. "I didn't even recognize you. I thought that was the horse trailer. Why didn't you come down there?"

"I go wherever the horse tells me to," I say. "You should have seen Aidan's face."

Tom and Dave are already unpacking the horses, and we interrupt for introductions. Rose shakes hands, says, "You guys ready for a cold one?"

She runs down and brings our truck up beside the Fish and Game trucks. She has two coolers, one full of beer and pop, iced tea, lemonade, water, the other with huge submarine sandwiches, a variety for every palate. She has homemade brownies. Cookies. Chips. Salsa. Pretzels. Tom and Dave, having never seen her in action, can hardly believe it.

As the driver, Tom has to turn down the beer, but Rose gets him something else. Dave takes the boys on rides around the parking lot on Gus. Tom and I go through the loads they've stacked into the pickup, taking the last of my stuff out of panniers and saddlebags. I carry my dry bags to our truck.

We tell stories, have happy hour, hors d'oeuvres, dinner, and dessert all in a half hour or so. The boys dance around me, the horses. They get another ride on Gus. Aidan wants to meet all the horses, and as we approach Tom's, tied to the front bumper of the truck, I tell him how to let her know he's coming, but she blows up anyway, maybe not quite sure what to make of this tiny horseman. She rears and snorts, hooves scrambling against pavement. Tom jerks up, but I already have Aidan in my arms, backing away. Tom's horse quiets, and I whisper, "They're big, they're dumb, and . . ."

"What?" Aidan says.

I shake my head. "Never mind."

We watch Tom and Dave trailer the horses, Tucker throwing his weight around, Tom having to slap him on the rear with a rope end to get him in. Aidan whispers, "That's mean."

It's late, and they still have to get to Choteau. Rose pushes more drinks, more food, and we have another round of handshakes. They thank me for taking such good care of their fish, and we watch them drive off.

Then it's just me and Rose, Nolan, and Aidan. The boys show me the great sticks they've found. I can't keep from touching them, rubbing heads, squeezing shoulders. "I've got a few things for you guys," I say, and open the straps on the blue dry bag, pull out the savage wear, their medicine bags.

Waiting is impossible. I slide the moccasins on their feet, breathe a sigh of relief as each fits perfectly. I wrap their legs in the long tops, thread the laces around their calves, tie them tight. They pull the vests over their heads, thread the knives and medicine bags onto their belts. True savages at last, they leap through the forest, feeling the sticks and needles through the thin layer of leather over their bare feet, the soil and duff, the years of collected fall from the trees.

Nolan, I'm sure, imagines every second of his lost weeks in the wilderness. Aidan leaps through the Elven strongholds of Rivendell, felling Orcs like cordwood. I stand beside Rose, the two of us smiling as we watch the two of them, our great good fortune.

Chasing their own rockets, reveling in the airy lightness of their steps, the feel of speed, of nearly flying, Nolan leaps over a log, brandishing his best stick and shouting. Aidan runs beside him, cackling with laughter, the best sound in the world. Better than the bugling of elk, the whooping whistle of air through a snipe's tail, the mournful howl of wolves—all sounds that, in time, they will have their chance to know.

Their laughter retreats after them through the trees, and I say, "God, I missed that."

Rose nods. "We always will," she says, and I find myself standing at the center of my life, one already so full, the regrets few and far between, little eddies among the main flow, none that haunt me, and none, not a single one, about any day I have spent in the wilderness.

I begin to call the boys in, say it's time for the four of us to head home, but after filling my lungs to speak, I fall silent. Yes, it's true, we all have to die, but not you two, never you two, not on my watch.

I let my air out and stand a moment more, watching them slip wild through the trees.

This. This is who I am.

Epilogue

Seaside, Oregon, and back
January 2009

Four years after tending grayling along the North Fork, I'm teaching in Pacific University's M.F.A. program on the west coast of Oregon, a great two-week winter gig by the storm-thrashed Pacific. I have my routines established, walking through the empty town before dawn, rain misting down, the surf crashing cold, to the city pool, where I swim a couple of miles, then take a long loop north out of town to have the walk back along that deserted stretch of beach as the day lightens. Inexplicably, the last mile of that walk one morning stretches out as long and as staggering as any of the worst of my egg missions along the Sun. Sweat soaked and exhausted, I pull myself up the five flights of stairs to my motel room, peel off my rain gear, skin myself out of my shirt, as clinging and as soaked as if I'd worn it into the pool.

Minutes later I'm picking myself up off the floor, won-

dering how I'd gotten there, why I'd been out cold. My own
Ozzie Smith flip. I pull myself to my bed, the phone there,
call a friend I'd talked into teaching for just this one semes-
ter, and ask him to come over, something's not right. I have
to get up and walk across the room to unlock the door,
make it back to my bed, a journey twice as steep as the Hill
of Doom.

When Mark blows in, he finds no grizzlies, no torn-open
elk calves. Only me, sitting up on my bed, shirtless, saying
something's going on. He checks my wrist, then my neck,
but can find no pulse. "Far as I can tell," he says, "you're
dead."

We go over symptoms: no pain, no arm tingling, nothing
but the sweat, this winding down like a clock. We guess
we'll have to call an ambulance. When that crew arrives,
they do find my pulse, but barely, straggling along at twenty-
two beats a minute. I'm unconscious by the time I reach the
hospital, and for the whole ambulance run over the mountains to Portland, the surgery there, the stent slipped in.

My father, beyond freeing me to run into that pond, has
also passed along his family's heart. A tear in an artery wall,
some overzealous clotting, a complete blockage. A heart
attack. The big one. Me. In an oceanside Best Western. No
one could have been more surprised.

When I wake, Rose is in the Portland hospital room,
waiting. I can't imagine how she'd been transported out so
quickly. As she puts the timeline together for me, out for
fourteen hours, not two, I ask first to call the boys, say, "They
must be so scared."

"Daddy, is it true that we all have to die?" And the next

line, "I closed my eyes and when I looked / Your name was in the memorial book / And what had become of all the things we planned?"

But Rose tells me I'd called already, the first instant I first woke up, that though I'd made little sense, I'd insisted. I have no recollection of being awake before.

When the doctor who put the stent into my heart checks on me the following day, I tell him I'm a little torqued that thirty years of swimming, of hauling myself up and down mountains, hasn't done a thing for me. "Oh, no," he answers, his accent clipped, "your arteries are supple, your heart is big. Without your mountains, you would be dead now."

I couldn't agree more.

9/16